THE UNLIMITED YOU

Don Clowers

DEDICATION

I would like to dedicate this book to my lovely wife, Sharon. I compare her to the woman whom Solomon spoke of in the 31st chapter of Proverbs. He said that a good wife is worth more than precious gems. Sharon has been a jewel both to me and our children. She has been and continues to be a woman of great strength and dignity. When she speaks, her words are words of wisdom and Godly kindness. Our children bless and admire her; and so do I.

In the years which I travelled as an evangelist, Sharon was most supportive of my vision and ministry. This made it easier to go and fulfill my call. After 20 years of ministering around the world, God called me to Pastor. She adjusted once again and has been by my side, holding me up and helping to bring the vision that

God has given me to pass. There are many great women in the world; but, in my eyes, Sharon is the greatest of them all.

I want to give special thanks to my secretary, Regina Chappell, who has worked so diligently on this book. She has spent countless hours typing and retyping the manuscript, having each part completed when it was always needed "yesterday." Her unfailing enthusiasm and dedication have been such a blessing and inspiration to me.

I would also like to thank Dr. William Turner, a friend of ours who has stood with us during the hour of trial and test. I will always remember how he and his wife, Linda, have supported us. It is so good to have a friend that sticks closer than a brother. I appreciate the time and labor he has spent editing and correcting the grammar in this book. Dr. Turner, "Sharon and I love you very much."

INTRODUCTION

God has something special for you! Everything involved with it is found in the Word of God. It isn't just for the past or future; it is something that He has for you now. He is vitally interested in how you look, feel about yourself and others, talk, act, and believe; and He has given it to every born-again believer. That special "something" is the new creation in Christ Jesus; YOU!

His desire is and always has been for you as a Christian to have the best of everything. Before you can come to realize how much of God's abundance has been delivered to the body of Christ and how to appropriate it, though, you must first understand the magnitude of the price Jesus paid on the cross.

Come explore and discover what it is like to live in the **NEW DIMENSION.**

THE UNLIMITED YOU

TABLE OF CONTENTS

ISBN 0-914307-31-2

Printed in the United States of America

PO Box 819000, Dallas, Texas 75381

Everyone who has asked Jesus to come into and be Lord of his life knows (has at least a basic knowledge) that Jesus took his sin and paid the penalty for it by dying on the cross. Many people, though, do not fully realize and understand the dominion, authority, and position that Adam had before he sinned. Satan has attempted (and sometimes very successfully) to cause the Christian to have a very low concept of Adam with the resulting conclusion that life as a believer is only "pie-in-the-sky by-and-by." Nothing could be further from the truth. I believe that as this chapter and those following unfold before you, the Spirit of God will begin to rise up within you and show you Adam's original greatness before the fall and your present status as an heir of God. Comprehending what encompassed the "old" creation is crucial to living and operating in the "new." This chapter is not intended to fully examine every aspect of the basis for walking in the New Dimension. Many books could be written about each one, but my purpose is only to give you the highlights and help direct you in your own study.

God's purpose for creating the earth was for man to have a beautiful place to live. He wanted man to have the very best and all of his surroundings pleasant. He made man so that He would have someone on this beautiful earth to **love and fellowship** with. His design for man was that he not be inferior to Himself, but He made him in His own image with all of His qualities. (Genesis 1:26 & 27) This is borne out in the scriptures. According to Psalm 8:5-6, Adam was created a little lower than God Himself.

> *"For thou hast made him (man) a little lower than the angels, and hast crowned him with glory and honor.*
> *v. 6, Thou madest him to have dominion over the works of thy hands: thou hast put all things, under his feet:"*

In verse five the word "angels" comes from the Hebrew word **ELOHIM.** It is the same word that was used in Genesis 1:1, "*In the beginning God (or Elohim) created...*" The suggestion of the Hebrew is that man was created just a little lower than God. Adam was the pinnacle of creation.

ADAM WAS SPIRIT, SOUL, AND BODY

Adam was a three part being. When God put His life in him, he became a living spirit. His spirit was created to rule over the other two parts, the soul and body. His soul, made up of his mind, will, and emotions, was pure. His body was perfectly healthy. He was in God's class. He could communicate with God, and God with him. He was given God's power, ability, authority, and dominion; and told that he was not limited in what he could do on the earth but to subdue it. Adam was actually the god of the earth.

Giving man a will was an important part of God's plan. Without it man could not have made any choices and would have been nothing more than a robot or a puppet. Adam was not forced to love God by instinct. He had a choice to fellowship with and love the Father who created him. Everything that the Garden of Eden had to offer was Adam's except for one, the tree of the knowledge of good and evil.

> *"But of the tree of the knowledge of good and evil, thou shalt not eat of it: for in the day that thou eatest thereof thou shalt surely die." [Genesis 2:17]*

God was saying to Adam, "If you eat of that tree, you will be separated from me, and I will no longer be your life. You will lose the control that has been given to you over the earth."

GOD GAVE ADAM A WIFE

> *"And the Lord God said, It is not good that the man should be alone; I will make him an help meet for him." [Genesis 2:18]*

God gave Adam a wife. She was bone of his bone and flesh of his flesh; they were one. Both were complete and had no lack. God gave them everything that they could ever want. They were happy and fulfilled with God and all that He had given them. They were set up to live in this state forever.

SATAN TEMPTED EVE

Satan saw what God had done for man. He was angry at God, because he had been cast out of heaven. He wanted to get even so he went after the closest thing to God, **man.** Satan, in the form of the serpent, came to Eve in a very sly way. He knew that he must not tell Eve a lie at first but instead use a subtle approach until he could get her complete attention. He asked her, "Did God really say that you must not eat the fruit from any tree in the garden?" She replied, "Yes, we can eat any fruit from the trees in the garden except the tree in the middle of the garden.We are not to touch it. If we do, we will die." Satan then became very direct. He said forcefully, "That's a lie. You won't really die. Your eyes will be opened, and you'll become like God. You will be able to know good from evil." Eve then chose the word of Satan over what God had commanded. She ate of the forbidden fruit, and immediately her eyes were opened. When Adam discovered that he couldn't communicate with her, he ate of the fruit also.

When he did; sin entered into his spirit, his blood was contaminated with sin, and he became separated from God. He was no longer a spirit-ruled man; now he could only have direction through his five senses. Life had totally different meaning for him, because he did not have the inner Divine direction. Darkness had consumed him. He was no longer the *perfect son of God.* He had the knowledge of good and evil.

This was a dark day in heaven and on earth because of the type of man that Adam was. His body was made from the earth, but his spirit was in the image and likeness of God. The heart of God was hurt when Adam sinned, because He loved man so much. God had given His word, though. He had told Adam that if he ate of the tree of knowledge of good and evil, he would surely die. Adam did anyway, and he died spiritually. Not only was his spirit contaminated by sin,but his blood was also, and physical death began. *"For the life of the flesh is in the blood..." [Leviticus 17:11]*

Adam and Eve were ashamed. Before, they had not known fear, but everything changed for them. They hid themselves from God where they had once welcomed Him. In the cool of the day, the Lord called out to Adam, "Where art thou?" He replied, "I was afraid, and I hid myself." He was running and hiding from God. He had never done this before, but now that he was inferior and no longer in the same class as God, he had no choice but to react that way. He was just a human being without the nature of God. In all actuality, Satan had become his master. Adam no longer had authority over the earth. He gave it to Satan when he sinned, and Satan became the god of the earth.

MAN WAS DRIVEN FROM THE GARDEN

Man was driven from the garden, no longer permitted to be in this paradise. God said to Adam, "Living on this earth will now be labor for you, and a curse is on the ground and upon man. And now until your flesh dies, you will earn your living by the sweat of your face." Eve was told that she would have her sorrow multiplied to her in bearing children. (Genesis 3:16-19, paraphrased) By turning away from God, Adam lost everything, including his self-image.

God could have destroyed man and started over, but He didn't. He loved him so much that He wanted to redeem him and be reconciled with him. God had given His word, and He always honors His word. When He gave Adam dominion, He didn't take it away. Adam gave it away. God said, though, in Genesis 3:15, "....*I will put enmity between thee and the woman, and between thy seed and her seed; it shall bruise they head, and thou shalt bruise his heel.*" God's plan of redemption and restoration was already in effect.

Notice that the scripture said her seed. It is a known fact that a woman does not produce seed; it comes from the male. God was saying that Jesus would come from a woman and put the devil under his feet. Adam brought sin to mankind, causing him to lose his dominion, relationship, rights, and privileges. His sin produced poverty, sickness, and confusion upon the face of the earth. Jesus, as the sinless seed of the Holy Spirit, was the only one who could restore man's fellowship with God.

SIN ENTERED THE BLOOD

> *"When Adam sinned, sin entered the entire human race. His sin spread death throughout all the world, so everything began to grow old and die, for all sinned.*
> *v. 13, We know that it was Adam's sin that caused this because although, of course, people were sinning from the time of Adam until Moses, God did not in those days judge them guilty of death for breaking his laws, because he had not yet given his laws to them, nor told*

them what he wanted them to do.
v. 14, So when their bodies died it was not for their own sins since they themsleves had never disobeyed God's special law against eating the forbidden fruit, as Adam had. What a contrast between Adam and Christ who was yet to come!
v. 15, And what a difference between man's sin and God's forgiveness! For this one man, Adam, brought death to many through his sin. But this one man, Jesus Christ, brought forgiveness to man through God's mercy.
v. 16, Adam's one sin brought the penalty of death to many, while Christ freely takes away many sins and gives glorious life instead.
v. 17, The sin of this one man, Adam, caused death to be king over all, but all who will take God's gift of forgiveness and acquittal are kings of life because of this one man, Jesus Christ.
v. 18, Yes, Adam's sin brought punishment to all, but Christ's righteousness makes men right with God, so that they can live.
v. 19, Adam caused many to be sinners because he disobeyed God, and Christ caused man to be made acceptable to God because he obeyed.'' [Romans 5:12-19, TLB]

Satan, as the god of this world, is the one who causes fear, strife, discontent, floods, tornadoes, earthquakes, and any like problem. He kills, steals, destroys, harasses, and causes pain in the earth. His anger is toward God. He cannot directly hurt God, so he strikes at man, the closest thing to God.

> *"The thief cometh not, but for to steal, and to kill, and to destroy: I am come that they might have life, and that they might have it more abundantly." [John 10:10]*

This scripture clearly states who the thief is and what his purpose is. He is out to **kill, steal, and destroy**. When Jesus came, though, He made it plain what His purpose was; to *restore* man to fellowship with God and give him back eternal life. Jesus said, "I want you to have life more abundantly, more than just enough to make it. I want you to have the life of God **overflowing** from you to others."

The Greek word "abundantly" in John 10:10 is PERISSOS, which means superabundant in quantity or superior in quality. When Jesus restored man back into his proper position, He said that you won't have to live an inferior lifestyle. You can instead live a superior life in this day and time, because you have the quantity and quality to be unlimited in the NEW DIMENSION.

PROPHETS, PRIESTS, AND KINGS

After Adam fell, God's Spirit was not in any man on the earth anymore; therefore, everyone born from Adam was conceived in sin. He could not dwell in man until the sin problem was dealt with from heaven. God wanted to fellowship with man once more, and it was evident that He would; but until that time, special people were anointed to work, minister, and be a representative from God to the people and from the people to God. These people were the ***Prophets, Priests,*** and ***Kings.***

By having no direct relationship or communication with God, the people had no way to obtain true forgiveness for their sins. Sins could only be set aside or covered through a special ceremony on a certain day called the Day of Atonement. It was on this day that the High Priest (only) could enter into the innermost part of the tabernacle, the Holy of Holies, and offer a blood sacrifice on the mercy seat for the sins of mankind. Since there was no permanent forgiveness, this ceremony had to be repeated every year.

WHY THE VIRGIN BIRTH

In order to have legal entry into the earth and also be able to fulfill the requirements of redemption, Jesus had to be a son of Adam but be without sin. To be without sin meant that His blood had to be uncontaminated, unlike Adam's. This was accomplished through Mary's conception by the Holy Spirit while a virgin.

According to medical science it has been proven that the blood of an unborn child does not originate from the mother. It is produced within the fetus. Jesus could be part of Adam's flesh but not of his blood, thus the need for a virgin as the mother and conception by the Holy Spirit. He did not have a drop of Adam's blood in His veins; therefore, He was a complete human being without sharing in Adam's sin. His blood was pure. The blood of all men was affected by Adam's fall, and the cleansing of that blood could only be by the illegal shedding of Jesus' pure and sinless blood.

Jesus, as the lamb slain before the foundation of the world, knew His task and function before coming to earth. Sent by God to reconcile man to God once more, He set the perfect example. He fulfilled the law and became the surety of the new covenant. His works, as prophesied in the Old Testament and chronicled in the New Testament, are as unchanged as God. They give man, as they did from the days of Jesus' earthly ministry to the time that He returns again to earth, the way of life rather than condemnation.

> *"For God sent not his Son into the world to condemn the world; but that the world through him might be saved." [John 3:17]*

JESUS SURRENDERED TO GOD'S WILL

Before His death Jesus went to the garden of Gethsemane to pray. He knew what He had to face. He knew that He must accept sin into His Spirit. Sin had never touched Him. Knowing that He had to be separated from His Father and actually go to the pits of hell weighed heavily upon His mind. He had to pay the penalty of sin, shed His blood, taste spiritual death, identify with man, and become cursed before man could be forgiven and restored.

Knowing the extent of that penalty caused Jesus to be in great agony until the pores of His skin released sweat and blood; so much so that an angel had to come and give Him strength. He was struggling with the powers of darkness in the garden and did not want to be separated from His Father. He knew, though, that there was no other way by which man would ever be free from the curse of sin. He became willing to be that curse and said, "Not my will, but thine be done." When He left the garden, He came out the Master.

> *"And He was withdrawn from them about a stone's cast, and kneeled down, and prayed,*
> *v. 42, Saying, Father, if thou be willing, remove this cup from me: nevertheless not my will, but thine, be done,*
> *v. 43, And there appeared an angel unto him from heaven, strengthening him.*
> *v. 44, And being in an agony he prayed more earnestly: and his sweat was as it were great drops of blood falling down to the ground." [Luke 22:41-44]*

Jesus was ready to offer Himself as the **supreme sacrifice for man** and to identify with man's sin. To pay the penalty of that crime, He would go into the pit of hell for 3 days and nights. He knew He must do it alone. It was sad, because the disciples who had been so close to Him did not even realize what was taking place. Jesus went to the cross after being beaten by the Roman soldiers. God's plan was unfolding before the world; the great sacrifice was being made.

JESUS DIED SPIRITUALLY

Then a strange thing happened. Darkness came

from 12 Noon until 3:00 p.m.

> *"Now from the sixth hour there was darkness over all the land unto the ninth hour.*
> *v. 46, And about the ninth hour Jesus cried with a loud voice, saying, Eli, Eli, lama sabach'thani? that is to say, My God, my God, why hast thou forsaken me?" [Matthew 27:45-46]*

Sin entered into the Spirit of Jesus and His physical death began. When He cried out in verse 50, He released His Spirit to death.

> *"Jesus, when he had cried again with a loud voice, yielded up the ghost.*
> *v. 51, And, behold, the veil of the temple was rent in twain from the top to the bottom; and the earth did quake, and the rocks rent;" [Matthew 27:50-51]*

The veil in the tabernacle that separated the Holy Places from the Holy of Holies was rent. This was the place only the High Priest could go, and then just once a year. A human high priest was no longer needed. Jesus became man's high priest and mediator. Each believer had personal access and could now go directly to God. Yet the work was still incomplete.

JESUS WENT TO HELL

The Spirit of Jesus went to hell. The real Jesus was in pain while the body of Jesus was lying in the tomb. You can understand that His body was not the real

Jesus, just as your body is not the real you. Looking at Psalm 88, you can see the awful pain that Jesus suffered. It says that He went to the lowest parts of hell. This Psalm could not be giving reference to anyone but Jesus.

Jesus was now meeting all the demands of Divine justice. He was there illegally, though, because He had never sinned. Satan thought he was in control, but he was the one who was really in trouble. He didn't know what was actually taking place, but God did. It had all been hidden from Satan and his agents.

> "*Which none of the princes of this world knew: for had they known it, they would not have crucified the Lord of glory.*" *[I Corinthians 2:8]*

Colossians 1:26 says,

> "*Even the mystery which hath been hid from ages and from generations, but now is made known to his saints:*"

God had the devil right where He wanted him. Satan could not win, because He could not hold Jesus in the pit. Jesus would only have to stay until the Supreme Court of the Universe was satisfied.

JESUS WAS BORN AGAIN

On the third day the Father gave Jesus His life once more. He was reborn in the midst of hell.

> "*For unto which of the angels said he at any time, Thou art my Son, this day have I begot-*

ten thee? And again, I will be to him a Father, and he shall be to me a Son?" [Hebrews 1:5]

This was the day that Jesus was begotten by the Father. Jesus had been separated from His Father for 3 days. The Father said, "That's enough," and Jesus was reborn from spiritual death.

"I am he that liveth, and was dead; and, behold, I am alive for evermore, A-men; and have the keys of hell and of death." [Revelations 1:18]

Keys represent authority. Jesus was saying, "I now take back the authority which Adam gave to you when he sinned."

"And he is the head of the body, the church: who is the beginning, the firstborn from the dead; that in all things he might have the preeminence." [Colossians 1:18]

Jesus was the first person to be born again from spiritual death to spiritual life. Jesus went through the same death Adam went through. Adam committed sin; but Jesus accepted sin and laid down His life, and now all men who ***believe and confess*** that Jesus is Lord can be born again or made alive unto God.

EVERY PERSON CAN BE BORN AGAIN

"That if thou shalt confess with thy mouth the Lord Jesus, and shalt believe in thine heart that God hath raised him from the dead, thou shalt be saved.

v. 10, For with the heart man believeth unto righteousness; and with the mouth confession is made unto salvation." *[Romans 10:9 & 10]*

You see, Jesus was made alive unto God, justified, and made righteous. In the spirit you can't be made righteous unless you have been unrighteous.

"For Christ also hath once suffered for sins, the just for the unjust, that he might bring us to God, being put to death in the flesh, but quickened by the Spirit:" *[I Peter 3:18]*

Jesus was made sin with your sin. He was made righteous with your unrighteousness. He partook of spiritual death. He gave up His eternal life so you could receive it!

"And without controversy great is the mystery of godliness: God was manifest in the flesh, justified in the Spirit, seen of angels, preached unto the Gentiles, believed on in the world, received up into glory." *[I Timothy 3:16]*

JESUS WENT INTO THE NEW HOLY OF HOLIES

When Jesus rose from the dead, He met Mary Magdalene. She wanted to hold on to Him, but He said to her, "Don't cling to me, For I have not yet ascended to the Father to sprinkle my blood in the new Holy of Holies. I must do this; go and tell my brethren that I ascend unto my Father. I am going to fulfill the Old Covenant; and when I come back, you can then put your hands on me." [John 20:17, Paraphrased]

When Jesus left her, He went to the new Holy of Holies and carried his blood there.

> *"That is why the sacred tent down here on earth, and everything in it-all copies from things in heaven-all had to be made pure by Moses in this way, by being sprinkled with the blood of animals. But the real things in heaven, of which that down here are copies, were made pure with far more precious offerings.*
>
> *v. 24, For Christ has entered into heaven itself, to appear now before God as our Friend. It was not in the earthly place of worship that he did this, for that was merely a copy of the real temple in heaven.*
>
> *v. 25, Nor has he offered himself again and again, as the high priest down here on earth offers animal blood in the Holy of Holies each year.*
>
> *v. 26, If that had been necessary, then he would have had to die again and again, ever since the world began. But no! He came once for all, at the end of the age, to put away the power of sin forever by dying for us." [Hebrews 9:23-26, TLB]*

Now, it was complete. He was the High Priest. The New Covenant could begin to function. Jesus became the mediator between fallen man and the Father God.

"And for this cause he is the mediator of the

new testament, that by means of death, for the redemption of the transgressions that were under the first testament, they which are called might receive the promise of eternal inheritance." [Hebrews 9:15]

JESUS PREACHED TO THE SPIRITS IN PRISON

Jesus came back after He had been with the Father and appeared to the disciples. He let them see and feel the scars on His body. Many other signs took place in that 40 days. After Jesus had been to the Father and sprinkled His blood on the mercy seat, He could then descend to paradise, the place where the spirits go of those who died believing in the promise. Jesus went to these saints and told them of their redemption; that the sin problem was dealt with. Their sins were not only covered, but they were done away with. They could now be released.

JESUS CARRIED THE OLD COVENANT SAINTS TO HEAVEN

"Wherefore he saith, When He ascended up on high, he led captivity captive, and gave gifts unto men.
v. 9, (Now that he ascended, what is it but that he also descended first into the lower parts of the earth?)" [Ephesians 4:8 & 9]

In Acts 1:9-11, Jesus was caught up in a cloud. All of

His work on earth was finished. He now sits at the Father's right hand.

> *"And every priest standeth daily ministering and offering oftentimes the same sacrifices, which can never take away sins:*
> *v. 12, But this man, after he had offered one sacrifice for sins for ever, sat down on the right hand of God;" [Hebrews 10:11-12]*

JESUS IS NOW IN THE PRESENCE OF GOD FOR YOU

It was no longer a shadow or a type; the supreme sacrifice had been made. Now He is in heaven appearing in the presence of God for you. How thrilling it is to think that Jesus is waiting there for a message from you to present to the Father.

> *"For Christ is not entered into the holy places made with hands, which are the figures of the true; but into heaven itself, now to appear in the presence of God for us:" [Hebrews 9:24]*

It is now possible for any man, woman, or child to come to God through Jesus Christ. No longer does anyone need to make a sacrifice to come to God or have a priest to go for him. The middle wall of partition has been torn down, and God's life is in you when you are born again.

I believe that the sequence of events which I have described in this first chapter have been absolutely necessary for you to see yourself with complete authority; completely restored with peace of mind; with power over sickness, pain, poverty; and knowing that you are no longer under the curse. Jesus was cursed for you. This should make the following chapters more meaningful to you and make righteousness easier to understand. As you read through the entire book, you will begin to take the limits off of yourself and be free to operate in the New Creation!

Chapter 2

WALKING IN RIGHTEOUSNESS

As I have ministered both in my own church and others, I have found that too many Christians have feelings of being powerless and worthless, because they have seen themselves as Satan wants them to. It is sad to say that, but it is true. They are born again and saved from hell but do not understand that they are saved from hell on earth. They live under condemnation, guilt, and rejection; never realizing that Jesus took the curse of those things for them at Calvary.

> *"Christ hath redeemed us from the curse of the law, being made a curse for us: for it is written, Cursed is every one that hangeth on a tree:" [Galatians 3:13]*

You no longer have to live a life of defeat or be unfulfilled. Jesus bought those things which would cause you to fail with His blood. He paid every penalty for you, and you are free from all the bondages of your past and/or present.

Jesus became a curse for you. All of the sin penalties that man had to come upon Him because of Adam's sin was dealt with on the cross. As a result, the Old Covenant law is not for the righteous. (I Timothy 1:9-10) You have been reconciled to God by Jesus Christ and saved by the grace of God, or rather, faith in that grace. Put all feelings of failure behind you. Don't hold on to them. **You are not a failure anymore, because you have been redeemed from it!**

Any feeling of rejection has to go; Jesus has not rejected you. You may have been rejected as a child by your parents and given no affection in your home. You may not know who your real mother or father is. You may have been abused as a child or had a bad marriage and feel totally inadequate to function as a normal human being. You may not be able to hold down a job or have close friends, because, as a defense mechanism, you reject others for fear of them rejecting you first. Man may have rejected you — but God hasn't. Jesus said, *"Come unto me, all ye that labour and are heavy laden, and I will give you rest." [Matthew 11:28]*

JESUS CARRIED YOUR GRIEF

Jesus was rejected and despised for you. He redeemed you from failure and rejection!!!

"He is despised and rejected of men; a man of sorrows, and acquainted with grief: and we hid as it were our faces from him; he was despised, and we esteemed him not.
v. 4, Surely he hath borne our griefs and carried our sorrows..." [Isaiah 53:3 & 4]

Are you grieving over a loved one or something which you may have lost? Well, Jesus has been there, too. You have just read where He was rejected, was acquainted with grief, and that He bore your *griefs and sorrows.* Let Him carry them instead of you. You may say to me, "But Pastor, you don't understand." It is true that I may not, but Jesus does.

Let me share an experience with you to give you something to identify with if you have lost someone that you love. On June 1, 1982, my 15 year old son, Jeff, was electrocuted and went home to be with the Lord. Oh, how it hurt. The pain and sorrow that Sharon and I felt were almost more than we could bear. Jeff was everything that you could want in a son: handsome, bright, loving, kind, and obedient. He had felt a call into the ministry; now he was gone from this life forever. We knew that we could neither see nor touch him here again and would not have the pleasure of watching him grow up to accomplish the goals which he had set in life. Because we are human, there was a natural tendency to grieve and reject the fact that he was really gone. Letting go was difficult. Little by little, though, we began to turn loose.

The funeral was a very different one from what you might expect. Instead of my wife and I weeping, we began to sing songs of praise to God as did everyone there. Phil Driscoll played his trumpet and ministered through the gifts of the Spirit. I ministered, along with several of my friends, a message of triumph and life. An altar call was given, and several people accepted Jesus as their Savior. People were mightily moved by the Spirit and continue to tell me that it was the most anointed funeral they had ever attended. God's presence gave us supernatural strength and comfort when we needed it so badly.

As the shock of his going home began to wear off, and the reality of it set in, we had to put ourselves totally in God's hands. T.L. Osborn called my wife and me with words of truth and comfort. He said to us, "Don't ask why; you will only be asking for an argument." What words of wisdom we received, and we accepted them. There were many times when we cried, but we always prayed in tongues or sang praises to

God. Something positive always came out of our mouths. His strength and the knowledge that He carried our grief helped us through many rough days.

There were also times when a number of families close to us in our church left, which added to our pain. It would have once again been easy to grieve and become bitter, but we chose to praise and worship God instead. We walked and overcame one day at a time. Wherever you are, if you are grieving, **stop**! Walk in your righteousness today. Tomorrow, do the same. In this way, life will be worth living. We would have made it had we not known that Jesus carried our griefs, but the road back would have been much more tortuous and difficult. The fact is, though, that we did and are making it, and ***so can you!***

RIGHTEOUSNESS IS A FREE GIFT

Jesus was made sin for your sin that you might be made righteous. It is a free gift, yet many people have a difficult time accepting the fact that God will give them something free. They feel that they must earn salvation by doing some type of works to merit God's blessings. No, His grace is sufficient. He created you to love you and give you His best, not because of what you can do.

> *"For he hath made him to be sin for us, who knew no sin; that we might be made the righteousness of God in him." [II Corinthians 5:21]*

The old spelling of **righteousness** was the word

"rightwiseness" which means having the right wisdom for a situation or acting right. Righteousness also refers to the ability to stand before a Holy God with no condemnation or guilt. In the Hebrew it means to be straight in the way, not traveling sideways. Knowing and understanding that you are the righteousness of God can be the most powerful force in your life. It will cause you to walk with a new boldness and confidence. You will no longer be troubled with inferiority or intimidation. Jesus Christ is your righteousness and your source of life. His **ability** for right living is your **ability**. When you understand this statement, you will walk with your head up and your chest out; not because you think you are better than others, but because you know that your boldness is God's boldness.

There is no lack in you. When you take on this image, those around you who have not recognized their ability may think that you are brash. They may say things like, "Boy, he thinks that he is better than others." They say this, only because they do not know their own rightstanding with God. Be loving and kind towards them but don't be intimidated by anyone or any situation. People who don't know who they are in Christ and feel inferior sometimes try to cover it up with a superior attitude. Therefore, they are abrupt, selfish, crude, annoying, and downright hateful. They are always bragging on themselves and putting others down which in no way represents the attitude of Jesus Christ. He is kind, affectionate, loving, giving, and compassionate. Righteousness never displays selfishness, but always builds others up and encourages them to do good and hold up their heads.

People who have never learned their standing in Christ or what true righteousness means have a real identity problem and are always seeking to be like someone whom they know and admire. They begin to take on many of this person's habits, try to get close to them, and hide under their identity. They cling to him/her until someone else comes along whom they can imitate or try to be close to. It is alright to become close to people and have some of their characteristics, but you **must learn to be yourself.** You are special and unique; you are made in God's image. Just because you are close to someone who is well known does not make you anything, so don't cling to that. It is walking in your righteousness that makes you somebody. You must have your own identity; and you can, because Jesus gave you His ability.

MY WIFE WAS DELIVERED FROM INFERIORITY

Several years ago, I first heard my wife, Sharon, give her personal testimony. She began with her childhood and told how she was always quiet at home, school, church, or wherever she went. She was very introverted and easily intimidated by others. When we were dating, she did very little talking; and even after we were married, she remained very shy.

As we travelled from church to church, she had no desire to be, and in fact, refused to be on the stage with me at all. After a year we had our first child, and Sharon wrapped herself up in our daughter. The second and third child soon followed. As a result, she had to remain home all of the time. She relied on me quite a bit; and since I was gone an average of 24 days a month, any situation was difficult because of her inability to communicate. When our fourth child came, Sharon really had her hands full. I was still travelling and ministering while she was busy at home. She related how she depended upon my prayers for her and the children. When something went wrong, she always called me to pray, no matter where I was. Sharon felt as if her prayers were not enough; that she could not get through to God as well as I.

As the children began to grow and attend school, she had more time for herself. She began to study and meditate in the Word. By doing so she found out who she was in Christ. She said, "I began to realize that I was the righteousness of God; that I was created in God's image. I found that I could go to God just as well as Don and be accepted in His presence. I could get my own answers." Her entire life was changed.

I saw her differently, and so did many others. I had told her the facts of righteousness all along, but she had to discover them for herself. She is now the Executive Office Manager at our church. She teaches, ministers, and sits on the platform. She no longer feels inferior or is introverted but is very outgoing and can hold a conversation with anyone. She does not feel a calling to teach; only to share from time to time. She made the decision to look into the mirror of God's

Word and see herself as God saw her; not as she had been looking at herself. Now she is much happier and more fulfilled as a person.

DO YOU BELIEVE THAT YOU ARE THE RIGHTEOUSNESS OF GOD?

If you were to ask a group of people how many had ever heard a message on sin, no doubt every hand would go up. However, if you asked them how many had heard a message showing them that they are the righteousness of God in Jesus Christ, you would more than likely get quite a contrast. If I were to ask you if you are righteous, what would your answer be? If you understood what God accomplished through Jesus Christ for you, your answer would be, "Yes, I am the righteousness of God in Christ Jesus."

When the subject of righteousness is discussed, someone always brings up the verse, "*As it is written, There is none righteous, no, not one:*" *[Romans 3:10]* This is talking about your own self righteousness. It is true that you are not righteous in your own self, deeds, or merits. Another one is Isaiah 64:6, "*But we are all as an unclean thing, and all our righteousness are as filthy rags;*" That was true in the Old Covenant. People were not born again, and their spirits had not been made clean yet by the blood of Jesus, so they were as filthy rags. However, if you say that now, you are calling Jesus filthy rags, because your righteousness is by faith in the blood of the Lord Jesus Christ. Your righteousness comes from God, not from yourself.

Righteousness is neither a feeling nor an experience, but many experiences and feelings will come from knowing your righteousness. Your righteousness in Christ Jesus is not **based on your acts, but on your faith in His acts!**

YOU DESERVE GOD'S BEST

I am crucified with Christ (Galatians 2:20), Who was crucified. My old, unrighteous nature was taken to the cross. When I accepted Jesus into my life, I accepted what He did on the cross for me. Now I have His life and His nature. I am worthy of God's best because of Jesus. I will not say that I'm just a worm and undeserving of the good things in life. No, Jesus made me worthy. How do you think God must feel when you say you're not worthy when He states so plainly in His Word that you are.

There are those who feel as if they don't deserve a vacation or any other good thing in life. But through Jesus, they do deserve it. Others will look at themselves and have low self-esteem. They stay depressed and moody, always feeling sorry for themselves. They hold an image of failure. They say, "Well, that's just the way I am." **NO!** A thousand times **NO!** This is not the way you are — it's just what you have believed about yourself. **You are the righteousness of God.** When you see this image of yourself, you will change the old patterns of your life. You will not only reach higher, but you will also think more highly of yourself and never again be the old **moody**, grumpy person you used to be. You will stop your "pity parties" and turn your energy toward being like Jesus.

A person who is walking in his righteousness will get up in the morning, bathe himself/herself, and dress to look like the person on the inside. The inside person is clean, strong, and alive. You will want to comb your hair, put on nice clothes, etc. You will make yourself look nice at home in front of your spouse and children.

It is very important that you bring your entire body under subjection to the Spirit of God that is inside of you. By doing so, along with prayer and meditation in the Word, you will feel good about yourself. It is then that the natural light of Jesus will shine from you, causing others to behold the good things that are within you.

You see, the world's general opinion of Christians is that most of them are overweight, out of shape, lazy, poor, not always truthful, and have bad credit. However, this is changing! Look at what Paul had to say in I Corinthians 6:19 & 20, "*What? know ye not that your body is the temple of the Holy Ghost which is in you, which ye have of God, and ye are not your own? For ye are bought with a price: therefore glorify God in your body, and in your spirit, which are God's.*" Paul said to glorify God in it.

Your body, as the temple of the Holy Spirit, should not be defiled in any way. The word **defile** means to spoil, ruin, corrupt, or destroy. As I just stated that the world's general impression of the Christian is somewhat negative; what you say, do, how you act, and display yourself as a born-again, spirit-filled believer is vastly important to how quickly God's purpose on this earth is carried out.

Your role as God's Word on this earth is to personify Jesus. In the first chapter of John, Philip pointed Nathaniel to the person of Jesus. He told him, "Come and see; come and see." If you continually overeat, use tobacco in any form, drink alcoholic beverages, fail to speak the truth, gossip, or act in any way according to the traditions of the world, what is the person that you come in contact with to see? Does he see your priority as food, tobacco, alcohol, or any other negative influence? If any or all of these have preeminence in your life, Jesus cannot.

If you don't see the righteousness within you and act on it, neither will anyone else. If you defile your temple, you simultaneously bring doubt on the authenticity of God's Word in the eyes of others. The planted seed that grows into a born-again experience for an unbeliever comes from the spoken word out of the mouth of a true Christian. Make the seed that you sow or water able to be increased by God.

None of this is intended to condemn you in any way if you find yourself in any of these categories. If you are aware of it (them), and genuinely seeking God for deliverance, you are walking after the Spirit and not the flesh (Romans 8:1). As a result, others will see that and desire the righteousness that you walk in.

Take a look at yourself and what God has done for you through Jesus Christ right now and decide, once and for all, to bring your flesh in line with the Word of God. Walk in all of your righteousness. When you do, you will have no reason to feel uncomfortable, inferior, or out of place around others. You will be able to be the person God says you can be.

THE SOURCE OF RIGHTEOUSNESS

God is the source of your righteousness; He gives you His own. You have God's very own righteous nature, as I shared previously, in II Corinthians 5:21.

There are people who will look at others with special talents or dynamic personalities and say, "Boy, if I had his/her ability, I could really do something in life." Let me ask you this, "Why look at them?" Instead, look at Jesus and desire to be like Him. He lives within you. With His power in you, you are unlimited.

In the first chapter of this book I shared with you that all men were created with the seeds of greatness. Man was designed for success an great accomplishment. Because Jesus is your source, don't limit yourself by looking at where you are now or comparing yourself to someone else. Don't hinder those good seeds which are inside of you; let them grow. Become the person you want to be. Create the environment that you want to be in. *"But of him are ye in Christ Jesus, who of God is made unto us wisdom, and righteousness, and sanctification, and redemption:" [I Corinthians 1:30]*

RIGHTEOUSNESS COMES FROM WITHIN, NOT FROM YOUR WORKS

Some people try to clean up their lives before coming to God. They become very frustrated because of a lack of power to make the change. The problem is that they have the cart before the horse. The church which I grew up in taught that to be a righteous and holy person, almost everything was forbidden. We were told that a woman could not wear makeup or cut her hair, that no one could play ball, go to movies, and many other things. This was not righteousness....this was works. Works never has and never will make anyone righteous. It was bondage; laws that man has made, and everyone was trying to live up to them. This was not holiness either. Holiness is of the heart or of the spirit which you learn to walk in by overcoming the lusts and desires of the flesh. When God comes into your life, He gives you the ability to let Him live His life through you. It is His ability flowing through you that causes your life to be transformed from glory to glory.

RIGHTEOUSNESS PRODUCES ENTHUSIASM

> *"I have strength for all things in Christ Who empowers me — I am ready for anything and equal to anything through Him Who infuses inner strength into me, (that is, I am self sufficient in Christ's sufficiency)." [Philippians 4:13, Amplified]*

When you read and meditate on scriptures such as this one, you will become more righteous-conscious; more alive and aware of your potential. Enthusiasm will abound as you see your inner strength. **WOW!** Isn't that good news?

"But he that is joined unto the Lord is one spirit." [I Corinthians 6:17]

Christ is actually living in you. The spirit which you have received is not weak, inadequate, or defiled. It is God's Spirit joined to yours. You are one with Him! This part of you does not know any sickness, failure, defeat, or poverty; only success, because God is success. You do not have to believe anything negative that you've been told about yourself. You *are not* limited — you are *unlimited.* God wants you to be 100% successful. He wants you to live as free as Adam did before he fell.

> *"And of his fulness have all we received, and grace for grace."* [John 1:16]

In your spirit you have the identical measure of faith, power, and anointing that Jesus had after being raised from the dead. You have received "His" fullness. Think on these things, and doubt will have to go.

RIGHTEOUSNESS GIVES YOU ALL THE POWER THAT YOU NEED

> *"That the God of our Lord Jesus Christ, the Father of glory, may give unto you the spirit of wisdom and revelation in the knowledge of him:*
> *v. 18, The eyes of your understanding being enlightened; that ye may know what is the hope of his calling, and what the riches of the glory of his inheritance in the saint,*
> *v. 19, And what is the exceeding greatness of his power to usward who believe, according to the working of his mighty power,"* [Ephesians 1:17-19]

God is saying to open your eyes, see what you have, and learn who you are. You have been given the same power that He used to raise Christ from the dead and set Him on His own right hand, far above *all* principalities and powers. It is imparted to you at the New

Birth. How could you ask for more power? Become more aware of it instead of your sins, mistakes, and failures of the past.

> *"Herein is our love made perfect, that we may have boldness in the day of judgment: because as he is, so are we in this world." [I John 4:17]*

You are as He is. Your spirit is an exact **duplicate** of the Spirit of Christ. Under the Old Covenant, the Priest would go into the Holy of Holies once a year. The people went in by faith in the Priest who represented them. This was the type and shadow of what Jesus would do for you. Now Jesus is there. You're in Him; He's in you. You are there at the Right Hand of the Father in Jesus. WOW! As He is, so are you in this world. Do you understand this? If you can believe this, I guarantee you that nothing will ever be impossible for you; you'll never accept Satan's description of you as unworthy worm anymore.

As much as the seed of man determines the direction of life as a child is created, so the seed of the Living Word, Jesus, within you comes alive by an act of God at the New Birth. You are a 100% carbon copy of Jesus. You are taken from Him. God has not withheld His power and righteousness from you. Satan has only stopped you by his lies and deception. If you believe what he says, you are then limited by putting faith in those lies. Satan has also deceived many Christians into believing that they must pray for more power. The power is there all of the time. When you believe the lies of the devil, though, you do not recognize who you are and actually stop God's power and righteousness from working in you.

When you repent of your sins and acknowledge Jesus as your Saviour, He immediately becomes your righteousness. He is able to do that, because He took your sins on the cross. You can never be more righteous than you were the moment that you were born again. However, you will grow in the knowledge of this righteousness and how it effects your life. It is limitless, because it is God's. You will never run short of His righteousness. There is nothing you can do to earn it; simply accept it. Receive it as a gift from your loving, Heavenly Father.

RIGHTEOUSNESS AS ARMOUR

God tells you in Ephesians 6 how to dress for battle, yet many Christians leave part of their armour off and are defeated in battle. In verse 11, you are told to "put on" the whole armour of God. He's not going to come down from heaven and dress you. You are to put it on yourself. That part of your armour which you do not wear is where Satan will attack. It causes you to be "open game" for him.

> *"Neither give place to the devil." [Ephesians 4:27]*

A soldier would not think of going to war without being properly prepared. He would make sure that he had all of his weapons with him and be ready to fight.

> *"Stand therefore, having your loins gird about*

> *with truth, and having on the breastplate of righteousness;" [Ephesians 6:14]*

The breastplate of righteousness is part of your armour for protection against the attacks of Satan. In the Greek, the word **breastplate** is described as being in two parts - one to cover the breast, the other for the back and the hips to protect the vital organs of the body. I believe that this is significant to you.

The first area of the breastplate covers the breast or heart. You are to guard your heart with all diligence. Keep it clean and pure before God. Believe in your heart that God has made ***YOU*** to be the righteousness of God in Christ. This doesn't mean that you will always "feel" righteous. Righteousness is not a ***feeling*** — it's a ***fact.*** It's a ***fact*** because of the ***act*** of God. I'm not saying here that Christians will never make a mistake or miss it; they will. However, when they do, God has given them a remedy.

GOD IS FAITHFUL TO FORGIVE YOUR SINS

> *"If we confess our sins, he is faithful and just to forgive us our sins, and to cleanse us from all unrighteousness." [I John 1:9]*

For many years I read this scripture and asked, "Why should God be faithful to me to forgive me of my sins?" Then one day revelation came. God is not faithful to me — He is faithful to Jesus. God is saying that when you sin, go to Him, and He will forgive you because of Jesus. God is faithful to Jesus — and you receive the benefits of it.

As soon as you realize that you have sinned, confess it to God and repent. Run to Him, not from Him; His forgiveness awaits you. Immediately following repentence, you stand before God washed clean by the blood of Jesus. Likewise, you must also forgive yourself. God has forgiven you, so why should you continue to hold the past against yourself? Release yourself from the ***guilt.***

> *"There is therefore now no condemnation to them which are in Christ Jesus, who walk not after the flesh, but after the Spirit." [Romans 8:1]*

Don't let Satan condemn you. Many times people let Satan beat them over the head because of a past mistake or sin that they committed. Once you truly repent, you are restored to right relationship with God. Don't go back to it. Keep looking ahead at who you are in Christ and don't look at the past.

To help you understand this more fully, let me share a little story with you. Suppose Satan could stand before God (He can't, because, according to Revelation 12:10, he was cast down), and he knew of a sin that you had committed. He says, "God, I want to see the crime file on that low-down no-good John Doe. He openly sinned on such-and-such date, and I ***know*** that he is guilty before You." With a knowing look, God says to His angel, "Go get his file and bring it to Me." When it arrives, He opens the cover, looks at page after page, hands it to the devil, and says, "Here, look for yourself. John Doe saw his mistake and repented before Me. All I see is **RIGHTEOUSNESS, RIGHTEOUSNESS, RIGHTEOUSNESS!**"

John Doe is just like you when you look to God. Hebrews 4:16 says, "*Let us therefore come boldly unto the throne of grace, that we may obtain mercy, and find grace to help in time of need.*" Notice that the Word says that you can come in time of need. When you do, God's grace abounds toward you. So, if God sees you righteous, see yourself in the same way.

The other area covered by the breastplate of righteousness covers the back and the vital organs of the body. Without the knowledge of your righteousness in God, the vital organs in the body of Christ cannot function properly. When the vital parts don't function properly, the rest of the body becomes weak. When the body is weak, the work and will of God is hindered on the earth. So you, as a believer, must dare to take your place and believe that God's Word is true.

Righteousness is comparable to the merchantman seeking goodly pearls. He sold all that he had to obtain the pearl of great price. (Matthew 13:45-46) A pearl is made from a living organism. An irritant, perhaps a grain of sand, in an oyster is covered with layer after layer of an opaque substance until a beautiful pearl is produced. Jesus took the irritant of your sins and covered them with layers of His very own righteousness!

FOLLOW RIGHTEOUSNESS

"He that followeth after righteousness and mercy findeth life, righteousness, and honour." [Proverbs 21:21]

The world is looking for "life." Many turn to alcohol, illicit sex, or drugs; looking for happiness and meaning in life. However, you, who are in Christ, have the answer. It is your duty as well as your privilege to let His glorious light be revealed through your life so that others may come to know Christ and follow after His righteousness. As you follow after righteousness, you experience His life flowing through you. You will find His honour being bestowed upon you in whatever work you set your hand to. The honour which many people seek can only be found as they walk in their righteousness through the knowledge of God's Word.

DECLARE THAT YOU ARE RIGHTEOUS

As you open your mouth boldly and declare that you are who God says you are, you will find that you can do what God says you can do. You can be what God has called you to be. As you do this, some Christians become upset. They think that you are out of line; however, it is exactly in line with God's Word. It is agreeing with Him and believing that what He said is true, regardless of the circumstances. This is faith! And without faith, you can't please God. (Hebrews 11:6)

MEDITATE ON RIGHTEOUSNESS

In order to walk in the life of God, you must spend time meditating in the Word of God. Meditation has two meanings. First of all, it means to think about deeply and continuously. Secondly, it means to mutter, to study, and to talk. God told Joshua in Joshua 1:8 to "meditate" in His Word and to be a doer of It. He would then prosper and have good success. Everyone wants to succeed in life. You've heard it said, "Success does not come easy," and "You pay the price for success." In all probability, success does not come easily. I choose though, to believe it this way: "You pay the price for failure; you enjoy the price of success." If Satan is making you feel as if you can't succeed or giving you problems with feelings of inadequacy, build your self-image by meditating in the Word of God. Hearing the Word makes you more righteous conscious.

> *"So then faith cometh by hearing, and hearing by the word of God." [Romans 10:17]*

Faith comes, first of all, by hearing what God has said about you. Next, faith comes by hearing yourself say what God has said about you and others. I heard someone say that for every negative comment you hear about yourself, it takes 11 positive statements to overcome it. You are told to guard your heart. Be careful what you speak about yourself — and others.

RIGHTEOUSNESS PRODUCES AUTHORITY

By knowing that your righteousness is based upon an act of God and freely given to you, you can walk in your authority in Jesus' name. Your authority as a believer will be discussed in detail in another chapter. You must fully realize the fact that when you were born again, you became an heir of God and a joint-heir with Jesus Christ to all that the Father possesses. Joint mean a way in which two things are joined or sharing with someone else. Strong's Concordance says that a joint-heir is a co-heir, participant in common, heir together, an heir with. Meditate on this! It's a legal transaction that does not depend on how you feel, but on what God did through Jesus on the cross for you. God intends for you to walk in His authority **NOW** in this life.

God wants you to live by faith in His Word and not draw back, because He has no pleasure in those who shrink back in fear.

> *"But our way is not of those who draw back...and are utterly destroyed, but we are of those who believe — who cleave to and trust in and rely on God through Jesus Christ, the Messiah..." [Hebrews 10:39, Amplified]*

Tests and trials come to everyone in this life. However, you can come through every trial victoriously as you walk in the supernatural peace of God. You can rest in His strength. When your strength is gone, partake of His strength; when your love fails, partake of His love;

when your body is sick, partake of His health. God has provided the best for you.

REWARDS OF RIGHTEOUSNESS

God has provided many great and precious privileges for the uncompromisingly righteous. Here are a few of them:

> *"I have been young, and now am old; yet have I not seen the righteous forsaken, nor his seed begging bread." [Psalm 37:25]*

Neither you nor your seed will ever have to beg bread. God will be your Jehovah-Jireh, your provider, for you belong to Him. Remember that the gifts of God are not just promised gifts — they are offered gifts to you. Reach out and receive them from Him.

> *"He layeth up sound wisdom for the righteous: he is a buckler to them that walk uprightly." [Proverbs 2:7]*

Buckler in the Hebrew means shield, protector, and defense. God promises to give you sound wisdom and be your defense.

> *"By the blessing of the upright the city is exalted: but it is overthrown by the mouth of the wicked." [Proverbs 11:11]*

Cities are blessed, because righteous people live in them. Blessed is the nation whose God is the Lord. The place where you work is blessed, because the favor of God rests upon you and overflows to others.

> *"The fear of the wicked, it shall come upon*

him: but the desire of the righteous shall be granted." [Proverbs 10:24]

When you are walking in right relationship and fellowship with God, He will put His desires in your heart, and they will come to pass.

God hears the prayers of the righteous according to I Peter 3:12. God promised to deliver the righteous out **of all their afflictions.** (Psalm 34:19)

Although the surface has barely been scratched concerning the good things which God has in store for those who will walk uprightly before Him, I challenge you to study the scriptures to see more of what rightfully belongs to you. Make the quality decision to walk in all that God has for you in the New Dimension.

Chapter 3

YOUR AUTHORITY

From the beginning of time, God placed the ability to rule in man. He placed His abilities within man and made him to have dominion. Adam lost that dominion by willfully giving it to Satan. Adam was not deceived; he knew what he was doing. (I Timothy 2:14) But that's not the end of the story. Jesus, the second Adam, regained everything that was lost by the first Adam. Man can once again stand in the authority and dominion that God intended for him to have.

> "*And God said, Let us make man in our image, after our likeness: and let them have dominion over the fish of the sea, and over the fowl of the air, and over the cattle, and over all the earth, and over every creeping thing that creepeth upon the earth.*
> *V. 27, So God created man in his own image, in the image of God created he him; male and female created he them.*
> *V. 28, And God blessed them, and God said unto them, Be fruitful, and multiply, and replenish the earth, and subdue it: and have dominion...*" *[Genesis 1:26-28]*

Of all the creature that God made, man is the only one He made in His image. When I say man, I am speaking of mankind which includes male and female. God made male and female after His likeness. The Hebrew word, TSELEM, is used for image, which means "resemblance or a representative figure." God has made man to be His representative. Man was to go forth, carrying out the will of God on the earth. God told them take dominion over the earth, be fruitful, multiply, and replenish it. He made it possible for them to do that by creating the Garden of Eden.

God's will is for you to be fruitful in every good work, too. ***Expect*** to be fruitful in any work that you set your hand to do. God wants you to believe that He will bless the work of your hands **as you work for Him.** In Genesis 28, the word dominion comes from the Hebrew word, RADAH. It means "to tread down, to have dominion, to prevail against, to reign, and to rule." God told Adam and Eve to take their dominion. You, as the child of God also, are given the same authority in this earth. Are you going to take it?

Many of God's people do not take advantage of the authority that Jesus obtained for them, because they just don't know that they have been given power over the enemy. They have been told throughout their Christian experience that if it's God's will, they can have better health, a better financial life, etc. **It is God's will for you to have these things.** However, Satan has stolen from many because of the lack of revelation knowledge.

> *"My people are destroyed for lack of knowledge:..." [Hosea 4:6]*

Redemption and restoration cost God a great price — His Son. Jesus gave His own blood so that you could walk victoriously in the power of His name and do the works of God. Don't sit idly by and let the devil destroy your home, family, children, or nation. Rise up and use the authority that God gave to you!

DAVID KNEW HIS COVENANT RIGHTS

David, in I Samuel 17, knew his authority because of the Covenant he had with God. He trusted in the power of his God and was not afraid to walk like it or act like it. Look at the attitude of his heart in the following scriptures:

> *"Then David said to the Philistine, Thou comest to me with a sword, and with a spear, and with a shield: but I come to thee in the name of the Lord of hosts, the God of the armies of Israel, whom thou has defied.*
> *V. 46, This day will the Lord deliver thee into mine hand; and I will smite thee, and take thine head from thee; and I will give the carcasses of the host of the Philistines this day unto the fowls of the air, and to the wild beasts of the earth; that all the earth may know that there is a God in Israel.*
> *V. 47, And all this assembly shall know that the Lord saveth not with sword and spear: for the battle is the Lord's, and he will give you into our hands.*
> *V. 48, And it came to pass, when the Philistine arose, and came and drew nigh to meet David, that David hasted, and ran toward the army to meet the Philistine." [I Samuel 17:45-48]*

In verse 46 you read that David desired to see the enemy slain, because he was making a mockery of God. David said, "*I will slay you so that all the earth may know that there is a God in Israel.*" He wanted the victory to give glory to God — to cause men to know the power of the Almighty. When you walk in your authority, it brings ***glory to God!*** He spoke out his faith in God. He gave glory to God for the victory that he already knew was his. He had confidence in his ability to fulfill his appointed task, because God was on his side. He would not fail!

David said in I Samuel 17:36, "*...this 'uncircumsised Philistine' shall be like the lion and the bear which God helped me to kill.*" David knew that no matter how big the enemy looks, he's not powerful enough to win over a man who will dare to believe in his covenant rights with God. He did not compare his size to that of the giant. He, instead, compared the giant to God's size. He didn't think that Goliath was too big to hit; rather, he was too big to miss! David ran toward the enemy and slew him, because he dared to walk in the authority which God had given him. He did all this under the Old Covenant. Today, you have a new and better Covenant with God, sealed with the blood of Jesus. How much more will you slay every giant that opposes the will of God in your life.

TAKE YOUR RIGHTFUL PLACE

You may have situations which look impossible to you at this time, and you don't seem to know what to do about them. The first thing that you must do is look at who you are and the authority that you have. **Stop looking** at the size of the problem and begin to meditate on the size of God within you. As you become increasingly aware of your authority, Satan will begin to fear you instead of you being in fear of him. Believe and confess your authority in Christ instead of the problem. Let me say it again. **Confess who you are and that you have the same authority that Jesus has.** As you visualize this instead of living with the problem and allowing it to destroy you, you will live with Jesus and destroy the works of the enemy.

> "*...For this purpose the Son of God was manifested, that he might destroy the works of the devil.*" *[I John 3:8]*

By being depressed and discouraged most of the time, you do not magnify God. When you put your head up and refuse defeat, doubt, uncertainty, or any other lie of Satan, you will walk and talk like a true believer. God is glorified in you by your taking your rightful place in Him and walking in your authority.

WALK FREE

Satan will try to make you afraid of stepping out and acting on your authority. **Fear is perverted faith,** or faith in something bad or evil. Worry is meditating and thinking on the things that you don't want to happen. Break out of the grip that fear may have tried to hold you in. Walk free in the power of the name of Jesus and go forth setting other captives free! I've had people tell me, "That's easy for you to say. You have not been tormented by fear like I have, and I just can't get rid of it overnight." It may not change in your mind overnight; but when you accepted Jesus as your Savior, there was no more fear or darkness in your spirit. I John 1:5 says that God is light, and in Him there is no darkness at all. He is in you, so light is in you. Think of this instead of fear. When you walk in your righteousness and authority, you **cannot** fear.

> *"There is no fear in love; but perfect love casteth out fear: because fear hath torment. He that feareth is not made perfect in love." [I John 4:18]*

He is saying here that fear can only remain in you when you allow it to. When you do not discipline yourself to think the thoughts of God and speak the Word of God, you will not mature. Instead, you will fear. You don't have to, though, if you will develop your authority in love.

SALVATION GRANTS YOU FULFILLMENT

Under the New Covenant that Jesus assured with His own blood, you are saved. What does it mean to say, "I am saved"? Most people think of it in terms as an escape from hell. That's true, but there is much more to it than that. There are two Greek words in the New Testament used for saved. One is SOZO, and the other is SOTERIA — which means "rescue, safety, heal, deliver, do well, preserve, be (made) whole, salvation."When you accept Jesus as Lord of your life, he makes deliverance available, not only from sin but also from all the power of the enemy. There is health, peace, deliverance, safety, and preservation in salvation.

When you understand salvation, you know that you are an heir of God and a joint-heir with Jesus. As Jesus is, so are you. I know this may conflict with some theology; but as a joint-heir you are a co-heir or an equal heir with Jesus. You have been delegated authority to do the work of God and live life as God lives it.

> *"And if children, then heirs; heirs of God, and joint-heirs with Christ; if so that we suffer with him, that we may be also glorified together." [Romans 8:17]*

> *"Wherefore thou art no more a servant, but a son; and if a son, then an heir of God through Christ." [Galatians 4:7]*

Everything you need is there, but the decision is up to you whether or not you use all that is available to you.

> *"And he shall be like a tree planted by the rivers of water, that bringeth forth his fruit in his season; his leaf also shall not wither; and whatsoever he doeth shall prosper." [Psalms 1:3]*

If you will accept all that has been given to you as your inheritance in salvation, you will neither fail nor lack during times of trial and testing that Satan brings. You will prosper in everything that you do. Even though you may be experiencing difficulties, you will not wither because of your faith in God. You will not give in to the problem or circumstance but will see God's Word and your rights as a believer. You will stand until you see them all dealt with in the physical realm.

You have a right through the blood of Jesus to experience these blessings from God in this life. Lay hold of them and see them come to pass in your life. You don't have to wait until you get to heaven to operate in His abundance. It is yours now in salvation.

THE AUTHORITY OF JESUS

> *"When Jesus had finished saying these things, the crowds were amazed at his teaching, because he taught them as one who had authority, and not as their teachers of the law." [Matthew 7:28 & 29, NIV]*

Jesus knew who He was. He knew His mission on the earth and the power that His Father God had invested in Him. Do you know who **YOU** are in Christ? Do you know the mission that God wants **YOU** to do? Do you realize the power of the ***Limitless Christ*** inside of **YOU?** People notice something different about the man or woman who walks in their authority. Matthew 7:28 says that the crowds were amazed at Jesus' teaching, because He taught as one who had authority. People can sense if their teachers are just talking from head knowledge or if they speak with authority.

The Greek word for authority in Matthew 7:28 is EXOUSIA. From Strong's Concordance it carries the meaning of "privilege, force, freedom, power, right, and to take control of." Webster's dictionary defines it as "the power or right to give commands, enforce obedience, take action, or make final decisions; power or influence resulting from knowledge, prestige, etc.; power as delegated to another." Jesus knew who had delegated His authority to Him. It came straight from Heaven, from the God of the Universe. As a result He could walk in boldness and confidence. He could speak with authority...knowing that what He spoke would come to pass.

> *"All the people were amazed and said to each other, What is this teaching? With authority and power he gives orders to evil spirits and they come out!*
> *v. 37, And the news about Him spread throughout the surrounding area."*
> *[Luke 4:36 & 37, NIV]*

In Mark 4:39, Jesus exercised His authority over the storm on the sea. He said, "*Peace, be still,*" and the wind and waves obeyed. Remember, Jesus said in John 14:12 that the works He did, you could do and even greater works than those. Take Him at His Word — trust Him. There are no limits to the man who will choose to walk in all that God has given to him.

WHERE DOES YOUR AUTHORITY COME FROM?

Many Christians today will agree that Jesus had authority and did great miracles. They say, though, "That was Jesus — not me, He was the son of God.

Sure, **HE** could do miracles," or "That was for the apostles in the New Testament, but no one can do those things anymore." Do you read anywhere in the Bible where God said that you could not do those things anymore, or that it was just for a particular time? **No,** it's not there; and just because the New Testament prophets died, they did not take the power of God to heaven with them. You have been given the same power that raised Jesus from the dead. Remember, **YOU** are made in the image of God. When you become a new creation in God, His strength becomes yours. His power becomes yours — for you and God become united as One.

> *"But he that is joined unto the Lord is one spirit." [I Corinthians 6:17]*
>
> *"...as God hath said, I will dwell in them, and walk in them; and I will be their God, and they shall be my people." [II Corinthians 6:16]*

MAN'S DESIRE TO RULE

In the natural realm, men are always trying to rule over the elements of the earth. Here's an example. Doctors try with all their power to rule over sickness and disease in finding a cure. They search and search. Scientists gather as much knowledge as possible to send men into space and explore the unknown. A lion tamer gets into the ring with ten lions, all of them stronger than himself, yet he is in control. He cracks the whip — and they jump. **Why?** Because God has placed in man this ability and desire to rule and take charge. It has been that way since creation.

This desire can become selfish and is with many people, because they have never given their life and will to God. They are trying to rule from the intellect. As long as they do this, their motivation is not from God, and they will often treat other people badly. However, if you are born again and your mind is renewed to the things of God, this desire will still be there; but it will be balanced by the Word, prayer, and compassion for others.

If the natural man strives to walk in his instinctual ability — how much more should "the New Man," walking after Christ, function in the supernatural ability of God. The natural man is limited....the spiritual man is **not**.

> "*...If thou canst believe, all things are possible to him that believeth.*" *[Mark 9:23]*

JESUS' SINLESS BLOOD

As sin affected the blood of man, it was necessary for the virgin Mary to give birth to Jesus. He had to be a son of Adam, yet be without sin. He could be a part of Adam's flesh but not of His blood. God made the way for Jesus to be born of a woman, without the inherently sinful blood, and still be a complete human being.

> "*And I will put enmity between thee and the woman, and between thy seed and* ***her seed****;...*" *[Genesis 3:15]*

Science has proven over and over again that the

blood which runs in an unborn baby's vessels does not originate from the mother. It is produced within the body of the fetus. This can take place only after the male sperm has fertilized the ovum. As the fetus begins to develop, blood can be seen. The life then, or the blood, comes from the male sperm. The blood of the unborn child's mother does not pass from her to the child at any time. The mother is connected to the child by the placenta, a mass of tissue commonly known as the afterbirth. It serves as the structure through which nourishment for the fetus is received and wastes are eliminated. God was so unique in His design. What thought and brilliance He displayed as He created woman in such a way that the child could be nurtured by the mother, but not one drop of her blood would be interchanged with it.

To further show you how and where blood originates, look at an egg from a chicken. If it was not fertilized by the male sperm, all you would have is an egg with no life in it. However, after the male sperm has fertilized the egg, you can incubate it, and red streaks will appear indicating that blood is present. You can take an egg which has not been fertilized by the male sperm, incubate it, and nothing will happen. The egg will eventually spoil. The point again is that blood is derived from the male seed.

Mary, a Jewish virgin, did not have sinless blood. God chose her, though, and she conceived by the Holy Ghost. This union gave Jesus a human body with Divine blood, the only person who had pure and undefiled blood since Adam.

JESUS WAS A COMPLETE HUMAN BEING

"Forasmuch then as the children are partakers of flesh and blood, he also himself likewise took part of the same; that through death he might destroy him that had the power of death, that is, the devil;" [Hebrews 2:14]

The above verse says that the children (all human beings) were partakers of sinful flesh and blood because of Adam's sin. Jesus took part of the same flesh, but He did not have sin-contaminated blood. Moffatt's translation of Hebrews 2:14 says, *"He Himself participated in their nature."* The New Testament in Basic English: *"He took a body Himself and became like them."* The New Testament in Modern English says, "He also became a human being." In the Weymouth 3 translation it says, *"He took on Him a share of it."* In other words, He had the human body as all the human children, but His blood was divine and precious. There had not been any other like it.

THE SACRIFICIAL LAMB

Jesus was conceived by the Holy Spirit; God was His Father; and He was the perfect and pure lamb to be sacrificed for the sin Adam had committed in the garden. When He willingly laid His life down, He paid the sin debt. He went to hell for 3 days and nights. His sacrifice did away with every sin and all condemnation. He paid the penalty for **every** human being. All of the sacrifices that had been made before were only a type of what Jesus did on the cross. He spent time in hell so that you nor anyone else had to go.

> *"And they have overcome (conquered) him by means of the blood of the Lamb and by the utterance of their testimony..." [Revelation 12:11, Amplified]*

> *"And from Jesus Christ the faithful and trustworthy Witness, the First-born of the dead (that is, first to be brought back to life) and the Prince (Ruler) of the kings of the earth. To Him Who ever loves us and has once (for all) loosed*
> *v. 6, And freed us from our sins by His own blood, and formed us into a kingdom (a royal race) priests to His God and Father, to Him be the glory and the power and the majesty and the dominion throughout the ages forever and ever. Amen, so be it." [Revelation 1:5 & 6, Amplified]*

SATAN — THE THIEF AND THE DESTROYER

> *"The thief cometh not, but for to steal, and to kill, and to destroy: I am come that they might have life, and that they might have it more abundantly." [John 10:10]*

SATAN COMES TO STEAL

I want to briefly examine the three words: **steal, kill,** and **destroy**. Steal comes from a Greek word meaning "to steal small sums or petty objects; to take little by little." That's how the enemy begins to steal from you, a little here, a little there. Before you realize what he is doing, he has robbed you. Give the devil no place! Don't allow him to steal **anything** from you, no matter how big or small.

SATAN COMES TO KILL

The next word, **kill,** means "to immolate (sacrifice), or to slaughter for any purpose, to destroy the vital or active qualities of." It also implies "to numb." If you allow Satan to steal from you little-by-little, his next step is to attack your vital qualities. He'll try to hit you so hard that you will be left numb from his impact. Satan is not playing games; you are in a warfare. Your weapons are not carnal, but they are **mighty through God** to the pulling down of strongholds. (II Corinthians 10:4)

SATAN COMES TO DESTROY

The word **destroy** means "loss of well being, to tear down, lose, mar, neutralize the effect of, ruin, put an end to, take something useful and make it not useful." Satan wants you to look at the circumstances. He wants you to look at anything besides your authority. He does not want you to see yourself above, only as a loser. Satan's work is not pretty. You, who are walking in the righteousness God gave to you, have the answer. Jesus said, "*...I come that they might have life...more abundantly.*" *(John 10:10)*

LIVE AS GOD DOES

The word life in the above scripture is **ZOE** which means "life, vitality in the absolute sense." You can have "life" as God has it when you let His life be lived through you. Abundantly means "superabundant in quantity, superior in quality, beyond measure." Jesus came that **you** might have that kind of life working in you. The child of God's lifestyle should be superior in quality to that of the world. God wants you to prosper in all areas of your life. He is **for** you, not **against** you, and His desire is for you to live life as He does. Believe it — Receive it — It's yours!

THREE SOURCES OF AUTHORITY

You can walk in the authority and power of God because you:

(1) are washed clean by the blood of Jesus.

(2) believe and speak the Word of God.

(3) use the name of Jesus against the enemy.

There is power in the blood! There is power in the Word! There is power in the Name!

THE BLOOD

I want to take a brief look at each one, and I'll start by giving you some background information concerning blood. In the garden when Adam ate fruit from the tree of knowledge of good and evil, sin poisoned his blood and brought him spiritual death. All men, black or white, Gentile or Jew, are blood relatives of Adam.

Because they are, their blood carries the same sentence of death. Adam's body was also affected, because the body is given life by the blood. This is the reason that the flesh is called sinful flesh.

NOW YOU ARE SONS

> *"Beloved, now are we the sons of God..." [I John 3:2]*

It doesn't say that you will be sons; it says **now** are you sons. Walk like sons — live like sons. This same authority has been passed on to you through Jesus Christ, your Lord.

> *"Then he called his twelve disciples together, and gave them power and authority over all devils, and to cure diseases.*
> *v. 2, And he sent them to preach the kingdom of God, and to heal the sick." [Luke 9:1 & 2]*

JESUS GAVE YOU POWER AND AUTHORITY

Jesus gave His disciples both power and authority. The two words used here are different. The Greek word for power is DUNAMIS, from which comes the word dynamite. It means "miraculous power, implies a miracle itself, worker of miracles, power, strength, and mighty wonderful works." Remember the word authority means "the right to give commands, to enforce obedience." That's enough to make you shout! You have the dynamite, miracle-working power from

God and the right to give commands to the enemy to "back off" in Jesus' name.

You can see that this power is given to Jesus' disciples. Some say, "That was only for the twelve." Do you know what the word disciple means? It means "a pupil or follower of any teacher or school." Are you a follower of Jesus today? If you are, then you are His disciple today. You have the same power and authority that Jesus gave to them — with one exception. Your authority is better than what they had, because God lives **inside** of you.

You have been sent by God to do His works. Those whom He sends, He also equips. You have been ***equipped*** with the ***supernatural power*** of God to do the works of God in Jesus' name.

> *"The Spirit of the Lord is upon me, because he hath anointed me to preach the gospel to the poor; he hath sent me to heal the brokenhearted, to preach deliverance to the captives, and recovering of sight to the blind, to set at liberty them that are bruised,*
> *V. 19, To preac the acceptable year of the Lord." [Luke 4:18 & 19]*

YOU ARE ANOINTED

God anointed Jesus to do His works, and He has anointed you. You are anointed whether you feel like it or not. The anointing is in you, because God is in you. This is not to say, though, that there are no special anointings. There are, and on special occasions, they will be felt by you for a particular time and purpose.

> *"But the anointing which ye have received of him abideth in you..." [I John 2:27]*

Here's an example to illustrate my point. Let's say there is a young couple who desires to be married. They go to a Justice-of-the-Peace or a Minister. That day things are going great for the minister, and he "feels" spiritual. So he performs the ceremony, and the couple goes their way, married.

Two days later, another couple comes to him to be married, and this time he doesn't "feel" quite so spiritual. He has had a hard day and doesn't feel like a minister of God, yet he performs the ceremony and sends them on their way, as married as the couple before.

Was couple number two any less married than couple number one? No! Why? Because the minister had a legal license to perform wedding ceremonies whether he felt "anointed" to do it or not. He had been delegated that authority by someone higher in authority than he was.

Do you get the picture? You have been delegated the **authority and power** to do the works of God today, whether you "feel" like it or not, by the blood of God's Son, Jesus. The One who delegates the authority to you is **Number One**. You can't go any higher than He is to get permission. He says to you, "Permission granted. Go in My name and do My works."

WHY SINLESS BLOOD?

Since Adam's sin defiled the blood of the entire human race, it took the unblemished, sinless blood of Jesus to make atonement for the sin of the world. Throughout the Old Testament there was the shedding of blood, a sacrifice of animals, as a type of what would be. This sacrifice looked forward to the perfect lamb, Jesus, who would die and shed his blood for the remission of sin. "*...and without shedding of blood is no remission.*" *[Hebrews 9:22]*

Jesus once and for all freed you from your sins by His own blood. His blood doesn't cover your sins, it washes them away. It leaves you standing clean before God, clothed in robes of righteousness.

Revelation 1:5 speaks of Jesus being the first-born from the dead. This is not speaking of physical death, because Jesus was not the first to be raised from physical death. Jesus, Himself, raised Lazarus and Jairus' daughter from the dead. The death referred to in that verse is spiritual death. He was the first — but not the last! I have a number in there too — do you? Because of that I have been given the right to walk in the authority of God.

THE WORD OF GOD

"For verily I say unto you, That whosoever shall say unto this mountain, Be thou removed, and be thou cast into the sea; and shall not doubt in his heart, but shall believe

that those things which he saith shall come to pass; he shall have whatsoever he saith." [Mark 11:23]

"So shall my word be that goeth forth out of my mouth: it shall not return unto me void, but it shall accomplish that which it please, and it shall prosper in the thing whereto I sent it." [Isaiah 55:11]

There is power and assurance in the Word of God. It ***will not return void;*** it accomplishes what it is sent to do. It is a fact that His Word never changes. What a consolation to know that you can trust and believe in God's Word every day for every circumstance. His Word is always the same, no matter what the world around you is doing. If you can see what I am talking about here, you will learn to trust His Word above all things.

GOD'S WORD NEVER CHANGES

As I look at society, I see things changing — some for the good, some for the bad. Your circle of friends may change. Your job can change. Anything in this world can change. I'm not against change, especially when it brings about positive results, but you can have something to depend upon that never changes. The only thing that is sure in this life is God's Word.

Many people believe (many times only by mental ascent) that the Bible is the inspired Word of God. They argue that it is what God has said but are unsure that it is what God is saying **now**. Compared to the number of people who are believers, few have had revelation of the power and authority in God's Word. They have not learned that they have the authority to use it in their everyday lives. They separate themselves from the Word of God and either depend on their minister for guidance or let things happen naturally. In Genesis 1, look at the power of God's Word. He spoke creation into existence; or when He spoke, the Spirit created because of the power in His words.

> *"Through faith we understand that the worlds were framed by the word of God, so that things which are seen are not made of things which do appear." [Hebrews 11:3]*

THE WORD IS TRUTH

God's Word is truth and everlasting, and He is faithful to It. He promised to send His Son, Jesus, and redeem man from the curse of the law. He kept His word and did what He said He would do. If you are a believer, He produced you as a son and brought you into right relationship in the Spirit realm by His Word.

> *"Of his own will begat he us with the word of truth, that we should be a kind of firstfruits of His creatures." [James 1:18]*

> *"Being born again, not of corruptible seed, but of incorruptible, by the word of God, which liveth and abideth for ever." [I Peter 1:23]*

DESIRE THE WORD

The Word of God should be a part of your total diet every day. As much as you need food for your phycial body, you need the Word of God to live life to it's fullest. Jesus said, "*The words that I speak, they are spirit and they are life.*" For your words to be spirit and life, you must meditate and renew your mind to God's Word daily. Let It become a part of you. Develop a desire for It as you would for certain foods.

> "*But he answered and said, It is written, Man shall not live by bread alone, but by every word that proceedeth out of the mouth of God.*" *[Matthew 4:4]*

Jesus said every word that comes from the mouth of God is important to you, so heed and hear His Word. Faith cometh by hearing the Word. Listen to the Word, read the Word, study the Word, confess the Word, and pray the Word until your word becomes His Word.

> "*Believest thou not that I am in the Father, and the Father in me? The words that I speak to you I speak not of myself: but the Father that dwelleth in me, he doeth the works.*" *[John 14:10]*

The Father and Jesus were one. He said, "*The words that I speak are my Father's words.*" The believer today should be as Jesus was. The word that he speaks should be God's Word. The action tht he takes is based upon what he believes to be true in the Word of God, not what he sees or feels.

WHAT IS THE SWORD OF THE SPIRIT?

Your words are filled with power when God's Word becomes a part of you. The Logos of God is what God has said. The Rhema Word is what God is saying to you and through you. It is revealed to you and therefore able to give life through you. Your words become the sword of the Holy Spirit. You cut through all the hindering forces and create from the spiritual realm into the natural realm.

> "*...And the sword of the Spirit, which is the Word of God.*" *[Ephesians 6:17]*

> "*Who being the brightness of his glory, and the express image of his person, and upholding all things by the word of his power, when he had by himself purged our sins, sat down on the right hand of the Majesty on high;*" *[Hebrews 1:3]*

All things were created by God's Word. He holds all things by His Word. His Word will endure and stand. Your words will too, if they are God's Words which come out of your mouth.

> "*Heaven and earth shall pass away, but my words shall not pass away.*" *[Matthew 24:35]*

GOD'S WORD CAN BECOME YOUR WORD

I believe what God's Word says and do not make excuses for It. I will not compromise. His Word never changes. In this generation His Word is as powerful as it was on the day that Jesus was resurrected. Take hold of God's Word and realize that it is not just written on a page with ink. His Word is your Word; and when there are circumstances, let the Word of God have first place in your life. Don't compromise. You are a winner. Take action; do what God's Word says you can. Don't back up because of circumstances but keep God's Word applied to your situations.

As long as you keep God's Word applied in a situation, you can win. You see, Satan is trying to steal the Word from you. If he can persecute you and get you to look away to other things, you will then lose your authority. Mark 4:17 says that persecution ariseth for the Word's sake. Realize that Satan is the one who comes to persecute you because of the Word. You're the one who wins, though, because you have been made a winner through the Word. As you believe, rely, and trust in God's Word, **all things are possible to you**!

DON'T DEPEND ON PAST EXPERIENCE

Don't go on past experiences of how you will live your life. If you are born again, you are now a New Creation. As a result of that each circumstance must be considered according to the Word, not what happened to someone else or what happened to you the last time. His Word will prevail when you trust, have confidence, and believe in it.

When Jesus was asleep in the boat and a storm came up, He was not afraid. As I stated earlier in this chapter, He knew who He was and what He had already spoken. Before He got into the boat He had said, "*Let us pass over to the other side.*" That is what He said and that is what He meant. When the storm arose, the disciples were afraid. Jesus wasn't, because He knew that the boat would not sink. He had already declared where He was going (to the other side). He spoke to the winds, they obeyed Him, and a calm sea was the result.

YOU ARE COMPLETE IN HIM

No matter what anyone may say, I urge you to meditate in God's Word until you receive revelation that God's Word is alive today. It is not limited. The only limitation has been in the minds of men, because they have been told that they are not complete and won't be until they get "home." As long as you believe this, you will never be able to operate effectively in the New Dimension.

> "*And ye are complete in him, which is the head of all principality and power.*" *[Colossians 2:10]*

This is either true or not true. I choose to believe that it is. You are complete in Him — He is inside of you **now**. Identify with the Word, light, and life rather than the darkness of this world and traditions of a religious system.

People will give you flack and tell you that the Bible is not for you today. Why should you believe them over God's Word? You shouldn't. Instead, as you take the Word and meditate on it, you will rule out all unbelief. There will be no more confusion, because you understand what the Word says and know that It is the final authority. One man said, "The Bible is the only book that you can read while it's reading you." The Bible reveals who you are in Christ. Read, meditate, and speak the Word of God, and you will begin to walk in God's authority and power.

THE NAME OF JESUS

> *"Wherefore God hath also highly exalted him, and given him a name which is above every name:*
> *V. 10, That at the name of Jesus every knee should bow, of things in heaven, and things in earth, and things under the earth;*
> *V. 11, And that every tongue should confess that Jesus Christ is Lord, to the glory of God the Father." [Philippians 2:9-11]*

God has given Jesus a name which is high above every other name. **His** name is above the name of **cancer**; His name is above the name of **heartache**; His name is above every **problem** in your life. They must bow at the mention of His name. Three worlds must bow to the name of Jesus: things in heaven, things in earth, and things under the earth. You, as a believer, have been given the legal right to use the power of that name and tear down the enemy's strongholds.

THE GREAT COMMISSION

The Great Commission, found in Mark 16:15-18,

tells you to *"go into all the world and preach the gospel to every creature."* Jesus said in verse 17, *"...In my name shall they cast out devils; they shall speak with new tongues; they shall take up serpents; and if they drink any deadly thing, it shall not hurt them; they shall lay hands on the sick, and they shall recover."*

Jesus said, *"In my name you shall do these things."* Do you understand what He said? *"In my name"* means in my place, as my representative. In my stead you go for me. You have been delegated the authority by Jesus to carry on His work for Him upon the earth until He returns. He will heal through your hands! He will speak through your mouth! He will set captives free through you!

> *"Behold I give unto you power to tread on serpents and scorpions, and over all the power of the enemy: and nothing shall by any means hurt you." [Luke 10:19]*

Jesus said, *"I give you this power."* Will you receive it? A gift is no benefit to the one it was given to until it is received. The word **power** here means **"the right to use power as received and when needed to destroy Satan's work."** To **tread upon** means "to have absolute mastery over." Satan is not to master you — you are to master him. **He has to obey you when you speak in Jesus' name.**

SPEAK AND GET RESULTS

Notice that Jesus said He gave you power over **all** the power of the enemy and that nothing (nothing is made up of two words, no - thing) shall hurt you. In the Greek the word hurt means "to do wrong, injure morally, socially, or physically." Nothing shall hurt you. That doesn't mean Satan isn't going to try; it does mean that you can exercise your authority over him and see him defeated! All power was given to Jesus, and He gave it to His people. I challenge you to walk in the power and authority that has been ***delegated*** to you.

Don't just repeat the name of Jesus; use it like you mean it. When you pray and speak the name of Jesus, expect results!

> *"And in that day ye shall ask me nothing. Verily, verily, I say unto you, Whatsoever ye shall ask the Father in my name, he will give it to you.*
> *V. 24, Hitherto have ye asked nothing in my name: ask, and ye shall receive, that your joy may be full." [John 16:23 & 24]*

What day was He talking about? The day in which you are living. He said to ask the Father in His name, and God will give you whatever you ask for. This is either true or not. There are no if's, and's, or but's about it. Jesus made this statement, and you can either believe it or not. You know, however, that what you ask the Father must be in line with His Word. When you come to the Father in Jesus' name, it is the same as if Jesus were asking the Father directly. When you understand how to use your authority in the name of Jesus, Satan and all of his demons will tremble every time that you do.

> *"And whatsoever ye shall ask in my name,*

that will I do, that the Father may be glorified in the Son.
V. 14, If ye shall ask any thing in my name, I will do it." [John 14:13 & 14]

COMMAND IN JESUS' NAME

He said, *"Ask it in my name, and I will do it."* This is a direct statement that gives you the right not only to ask but also to demand your rights in Jesus' name. When you look at the word, ask, in the Greek text, it also means "to demand." So as a child of God, demand that Satan leave you alone. A person who has his mind renewed to this fact is not limited to what he can have in this life. You can do anything that Jesus and the apostles did. God's power has not become limited.

"God forbid: yea, let God be true, but every man a liar;..." [Romans 3:4]

"Heaven and earth shall pass away, but my words shall not pass away." [Matthew 24:35]

Take your place as the Apostles did in Acts 3, where Peter and John met the man who had been a cripple since birth. He asked them for money. They told him that they had no money, but they did have God's power and authority. Peter said to him, *"I command you in the name of Jesus Christ of Nazareth, rise up and walk."* It does not say in the King James, *"I command thee,"* but it does say, *"RISE UP!"* This is a command. Peter commanded him to rise in Jesus' name, he did, and he was healed.

"Jesus' name has healed this man — and you

> *know how lame he was before. Faith in Jesus' name — faith given us from God — has caused this perfect healing.'' [Acts 3:16, TLB]*

Peter and John knew the power in the name of Jesus and used it. Hebrews 13:8 says that Jesus is the same yesterday, today, and forever. The power in His name has not changed since the book of Acts. God desires that you use this name for ever need that you may have.

ALL THINGS UNDER YOUR FEET

> *"And (so that you can know and understand) what is the immeasurable and unlimited and surpassing greatness of His power in and for us who believe, as demonstrated in the working of His mighty strength,*
> *V. 20, Which He exerted in Christ when He raised Him from the dead and seated Him at His (own) right hand in the heavenly (places),*
> *V. 21, Far above all rule and authority and power and dominion, and every name that is named — above every title that can be conferred — not only in this age and in this world, but also in the age and the world which are to come.*
> *V. 22, And He has put all things under His feet and has appointed Him the universal and supreme Head of the church (a headship exercised throughout the church),*
> *V. 23, Which is His body, the fullness of Him*

Who fills all in all — for in that body lives the full measure of Him Who makes everything complete, and Who fills everything everywhere (with Himself)." [Ephesians 1:19-23, Amplified]

V. 1, "And you (He made alive), when you were dead (slain) by (your) trespasses and sins

V. 5, Even when we were dead (slain) by (our own) shortcomings and trespasses, He made us alive together in fellowship and in union with Christ. He gave us the very life of Christ Himself, the same new life with which he quickened Him. (For) it is by grace — by His favor and mercy which you did not deserve — that you are saved (delivered from judgment and made partakers of Christ's salvation).

V. 6, And He raised us up together with Him and made us sit down together — giving us joint seating with Him — in the heavenly sphere (by virtue of our being) in Christ Jesus, the Messiah, the Anointed One." [Ephesians 2:1, 5 & 6, Amplified]

These scriptures tell you, as a believer, where you are. You are seated in a position of authority with all things under your feet. You are seated with Christ above all the power of the enemy. Don't let Satan deceive you; you have the power — he doesn't. Don't be afraid to take what belongs to you. If Satan has stolen your health, marriage, home, children, or finances, **confront him!** Walk with boldness and don't back down. Go after what you want. If you don't, you will never get it.

A football team has an offensive team and a defensive team. It is the offensive team that goes into the territory of the opposite defensive team to score points. You can't sit back and wait for things to come to you — you must take them. You are seated in a position of authority with Christ. You are restored to that position of authority where Adam was before he fell. I challenge you to start acting like you are in control instead of being controlled. You are made alive unto God so act like you are alive in God and become dead to sin. Satan and all his evil works can then only watch the unlimited Christ work in you **now** in the New Dimension.

Chapter 4

HEALING

There is a great controversy today over the subject of healing. Some people do not believe in it at all. Others believe that God can heal but are not sure if He will. Still others believe that as they suffer in sickness, they will become more like Jesus. Therefore, they don't dare ask God to heal them. There is an answer for this dilemma. The only truth is the **Word of God.** In this chapter you will find out what God's Word says about healing; and through the amount of knowledge of the Word that you believe and act upon, you **will be** set free. Expect to receive your miracle as you read!

HEALTH IS FROM GOD

If you were wishing the very best for a well-loved friend, what would you wish for them? The apostle John, writing to Gaius, said:

> *"Beloved, I wish above all things that thou mayest prosper and be in health, even as thy soul prospereth." [3 John: 2]*

John wished (or prayed) the very best for his friend. If sickness, disease, and poverty were of God, it's strange that John didn't write, "I wish above all things that thou experience poverty and ill health."

There are some people today who are permitting sickness, disease, and pain to torment their bodies, because they don't know that God has already made the same provision for them to be healed as He did for them to be saved. Hosea gives warning in the Word of God about not having the proper knowledge of what He has made available to believers.

"My people are destroyed for lack of knowledge." [Hosea 4:6]

God made your body to function properly. Genesis 1 describes man's creation. From it, you find 3 basic facts:

1) Man was created in the image of God. I can't picture God being sick or unhealthy. God is the Supreme Being, the One with all power and ability. Likewise, all mankind has the power and ability to remain healthy.
2) When God created man and woman, He blessed them. God did not create a sickly, puny, and diseased man. In Deuteronomy 28 you will find the blessings and curses of the law....Health is the blessing of those who obey the law — sickness is the curse of those who do not. When God created man, one of the blessings he received was health.
3) Upon viewing His creation, including man, God said it was "**very good.**" Disease is basically a malfunctioning of the normal health processes. Disease is made up of 2 small words — "dis" and "ease," which means **not at ease.** God would not have called His creation "very good" if disease had been present.

In the beginning, Adam was given dominion over all creation. He was to take charge of the earth (Genesis 1:28). When he disobeyed God and ate the forbidden fruit, he handed over his rights to Satan. Now Satan had the dominion that God had planned for man. Man was separated from God by spiritual death at the fall — introducing physical death. A direct result was that sickness, disease, pain, and decay entered the life of man.

HEALING PROVIDED IN THE OLD TESTAMENT

Healing was God's will under the Old Covenant as well as it is now the New. Look at these scriptures regarding healing in the Old Testament. One of the very first times it is mentioned is when God spoke to Moses and the children of Israel in the wilderness:

> *"If thou wilt diligently hearken to the voice of the Lord thy God, and wilt do that which is right in his sight, and wilt give ear to his commandments, and keep all his statutes, I will put none of these diseases upon thee, which I have brought upon the Egyptians: for I am the Lord that healeth thee."* *[Exodus 15:26]*

Before explaining what this verse is saying, let me clear up what it is **not** saying. This passage is not saying that God puts disease on people. Hebrew scholars say that the words "put" and "brought upon" in this text are in the permissive tense of the verb and would be better translated "permitted." In that case, the last part of the verse above would read: *"I will permit none of these diseases upon thee, which I have permitted upon the Egyptians: for I am the Lord that healeth thee."* God is saying that He won't allow any of those diseases to be put on His people, because He is their

Healer. Even if a disease were to momentarily be upon one of them, it couldn't stay in His presence. God wants His people to walk free from disease.

Later, in Exodus, God gave the Israelites more instructions, saying:

> *"And ye shall serve the Lord your God, and he shall bless thy bread, and thy water; and **I will take sickness away from the midst of thee.**" [Exodus 23:25]*

In the writings of Solomon, you can see this wonderful prescription for a healthy body:

> *"My son, attend to my words; incline thine ear to my sayings.*
> *V. 21, Let them not depart from thine eyes; keep them in the midst of thine heart.*
> *V. 22, For they are life unto those that find them, and **health to all their flesh.**" [Proverbs 4:20-22]*

You are to take doses of God's Word until it becomes **health** to your flesh. Solomon tells you first of all to attend to the Word; that is to look after it, apply yourself to it, and let it occupy your attention. You are also to incline your ear to the Word. The word incline means "to listen **and** take heed." Thus, you are to be *"doers of the Word, and not hearers only." (James 1:22)* You need to overdose on the Word of God. The good thing about overdosing on the Word of God is that it won't kill you — it will make you more powerful! It will make you well! It will make you successful in every area of your life!

God said, "....*I am the Lord that healeth thee.*" *[Exodus 15:26]* He said, "*I am Jehovah-Rapha.*" Jehova-Rapha is one of the seven redemptive names for God found in the Old Testament. These names reveal more about Himself to mankind, expressing His willingness to meet your every need. The names reveal God to you and point to Calvary, for this is the place where your redemption was accomplished.

The seven redemptive names for God are:

1) Jehova-Shamma — The Lord is there (present).
2) Jehovah-Shalom — The Lord your Peace.
3) Jehovah-Ra'ah — The Lord is your Shepherd.
4) Jehovah-Jireh — The Lord will provide.
5) Jehovah-Nissi — The Lord is your Banner (Victor).
6) Jehovah-Tsidkenu — The Lord your Righteousness.
7) Jehovah-Rapha — I am the Lord thy Physician, or I am the Lord that healeth thee.

As you can see from the 7th description, it is God's will to be your healer.

> "*Bless the Lord, O my soul: and all that is within me, bless his holy name.*
> *V. 2, Bless the Lord, O my soul, and forget not all his benefits:*
> *V. 3, Who forgiveth all thine iniquities; who healeth all thy diseases;*" *[Psalm 103:1-3]*

David was meditating on the benefits of serving God.

Here he mentions forgiveness of sins and healing **all** your disease. It is God's will to save you, and it is His will to heal you. Believe it and receive it.

HEALING IS PART OF THE ATONEMENT

> *"Surely he hath borne our griefs, and carried our sorrows: yet we did esteem him stricken, smitten of God, and afflicted.*
> *V. 5, But he was wounded for our transgressions, he was bruised for our iniquities: the chastisement of our peace was upon him; and with his stripes we are healed." [Isaiah 53:4 & 5]*

I want to examine this scripture closely. Isaiah was prophesying about Jesus on the cross. He was looking forward in time to what would happen at Calvary.

Verse 4, "*Surely he (Jesus) hath borne our griefs...*" The word borne means "to bear away, to remove to a distant place." Jesus bore away and removed your griefs. The Hebrew word for grief is **CHOLIY**, which means "anxiety, calamity, disease, and sickness." Jesus bore away all your sickness and disease at Calvary when He served as your substitute. "*....and carried our sorrows,*" verse 4. The word carries here implies "**substitute.**" Substitute means "**to serve in place of another.**" Jesus served in **your** place at Calvary, bearing your sins and your diseases on Himself so that you might be free. He also carried your sorrows. Sorrows comes from the Hebrew word **MAKOB** which is "anguish, affliction, pain, and sorrow." Verse 4 says,

"We esteemed him stricken of God and afflicted — but He was wounded for ***our*** *transgressions."*

It was the sins of mankind that held Jesus on the cross. Jesus was bruised for everyone's iniquities, the chastisement of everyone's peace was upon him, and with his stripes every person was healed. Isaiah was prophesying about what Jesus would do for all people at Calvary.

A trained Roman soldier lashed Jesus with the Roman scourge 39 times. Yes, 39 stripes were placed on the back of your Lord and Savior. I have read that there are 39 major diseases known to mankind. Someone might ask, "What does all of that mean?" It means that any sickness which attacks the human body has been defeated at Calvary. Jesus shed his blood for your sins first, that you might be saved. But He also took the beating by that Roman soldier so you would not have to carry sickness and disease in your body.

Jesus' complete saving work was accomplished 2,000 years ago on the cross. He bore your sins, sicknesses, and diseases — but you must appropriate your healing by faith. How did you get saved? By faith you accepted the work that Jesus had already done for you. Likewise, how will you get healed? By the same faith you had for salvation, you must accept the work Jesus has already done for you. You are healed! You may be thinking, "But what if I don't feel healed?" Well, what if you didn't feel saved? Would that make you not saved? **No!** Jesus said:

> *"Behold, I stand at the door, and knock: if any man hear my voice, and open the door, I will*

come in to him." *[Revelation 3:20]*

Your salvation isn't decided on the basis of how you feel but on the integrity of His promise. He said that He would save you, and you believed it. After all:

> *"God is not a man, that he should lie; neither the son of man, that he should repent: hath he said, and shall he not do it? or hath he spoken, and shall he not make it good?" [Numbers 23:19]*

Can't you see that it is the same way with healing? His Word says you were healed. Accept it by faith, just as you did salvation. You may say, "But my pain or symptoms are real." Sure they are. I'm not saying that you don't hurt when you know you do. I'm not telling you that the symptoms aren't there when you know they are. I am saying, though, that there is something more real than the symptoms. That something is what the Word of God has to say about the situation. God's Word views all as healed. Do you dare say anything less about yourself than what the Word of God says?

In I Peter 2:24, Peter looks back at the cross and makes this statement:

> *"Who his own self bare our sins in his own body on the tree, that we, being dead to sins, should live unto righteousness: by whose stripes ye were healed."*

Peter said, "*Ye were healed.*" It's already done. It was accomplished at the same time that Jesus bore away your sins at Calvary. It's now up to you to believe it and partake of it.

JESUS DOES THE WILL OF THE FATHER

The Old Testament makes it clear that God wills for His children to be healed and walk in health. The New Testament confirms that same desire. Many people pray, "Lord, heal so-and-so if it be Thy will." Jesus declared in Luke:

> *"And it came to pass, when he was in a certain city, behold a man full of leprosy: who seeing Jesus fell on his face, and besought him, saying, Lord, if thou wilt, thou canst make me clean.*
> *V. 13, And he put forth his hand, and touched him, saying,* ***I will:*** *be thou clean. And immediately the leprosy departed from him." [Luke 5:12-13]*

The Bible says that Jesus Christ is the same yesterday, and today, and forever. (Hebrews 13:8) He doesn't change. If He willed to heal while He was walking on the earth, He wills to heal today. Here are some other passages of scripture that tell of Jesus healing all who were brought to Him.

> *"And Jesus went about all Galilee, teaching in their synagogues, and preaching the gospel of the kingdom, and healing all manner of sickness and all manner of disease among the people." [Matthew 4:23]*

> *"But when Jesus knew it, he withdrew himself from thence: and great multitudes followed him, and he healed them all." [Matthew 12:15]*

"And Jesus went forth, and saw a great multitude, and was moved with compassion toward them, and he healed their sick." [Matthew 14:14]

Matthew also makes it clear that Jesus was the One whom Isaiah prophesied about when he said:

"When the even was come, they brought unto him many that were possessed with devils: and he cast out the spirits with his word, and healed all that were sick:
V. 17, That it might be fulfilled which was spoken by Esaias the prophet, saying Himself took our infirmities, and bare our sicknesses." [Matthew 8:16 & 17]

Jesus made it obvious that *"The Son of man is not come to destroy men's lives, but to save them." (Luke 9:56)* He didn't come to put sickness on people but to take it away. If sickness were of God, why would God send Jesus to take it away? The Bible says,

"....For this purpose the Son of God was manifested, that he might destroy the works of the devil." [I John 3:8]

God gives good gifts to His children. The Apostle James declares:

"Every good gift and every perfect gift is from above, and cometh down from the Father of lights, with whom is no variableness, neither shadow of turning." [James 1:17]

Sickness, disease, and death are from the devil and came into the world as a result of the fall of man. God's will is to heal all who come to Him in faith. He not only wills men to be well but also sent His Son to be their substitute, to bear their sins and sicknesses on the cross. Jesus hasn't changed. He is still healing people today, and I believe that these scriptures confirm that.

ORIGIN OF SICKNESS

Sickness did not originate with God and was not His plan for man. It will not be in existence at the final restoration of all things, either.

> *"And God shall wipe away all tears from their eyes; and there shall be no more death, neither sorrow, nor crying, neither shall there be any more pain: for the former things are passed away." [Revelation 21:4]*

If sickness is not from God, then where does it come from? The Word of God gives the answer.

> *"How God anointed Jesus of Nazereth with the Holy Ghost and with power: who went about doing good, and healing all that were oppressed of the devil; for God was with him." [Acts 10:38]*

This scripture makes it very clear that sickness is caused by satanic oppression. Notice that Peter said Jesus went about doing good and healing all who were oppressed of the devil. God's will was that those who were bound by sickness be set free.

Look also at the case of the woman in Luke

13:11-13:

> *"And, behold, there was a woman which had a spirit of infirmity eighteen years, and was bowed together, and could in no wise lift up herself.*
> *V. 12, And when Jesus saw her, he called her to him, and said unto her, Woman, thou art loosed from thine infirmity.*
> *V. 13, And he laid his hands on her: and immediately she was made straight, and glorified God."*

Jesus described this woman as *"A daughter of Abraham, whom satan hath bound, lo, these eighteen years." (Luke 13:16)* Jesus did not say that God had bound her; He said **Satan** had her bound. Many people accuse God of placing them on the bed of affliction. God is the answer — not the source of the problem.

Some say that their sickness is giving glory to God. They believe they are "suffering for Jesus' sake." No! They have it backwards. Jesus suffered for their sakes — so that they wouldn't have to. He was the substitute, not the cause.

If someone really believes that sickness gives glory to God, then why do most of them take medicine to get better? Why don't they ask God to make them doubly sick so that they can give God double glory? No! Healing glorifies God — not the sickness. This woman glorified God as soon as she was made whole. The healing brought glory to God.

Jesus gave further evidence of sickness coming from Satan when He said, *"The thief cometh not, but for to steal, and to kill, and to destroy..." (John 10:10)* Satan wants to steal your health from you. In the words of Jesus, Satan is a thief. Legally, when you turn your life over to Jesus, Satan is no longer your god.

> "*Who hath delivered us from the power of darkness, and hath translated us into the kingdom of his dear Son:" [Colossians 1:13]*

After salvation, your physical health is very important. Without it you cannot fully function in the service of God. Satan attacks you in subtle ways. According to the parable of the sower in Mark 4, he comes to steal the Word of God from you by affliction, persecution, lusts of the flesh, cares of this world, and the deceitfulness of riches. Many times people are able to at least have some idea that Satan is the one behind affliction, persecution, cares, and deceitfulness. They don't seem to realize, however, that what they put into their bodies directly determines how well or if they have the divine health that Jesus paid for at Calvary.

The body is a product of the earth and subject to both spiritual and natural laws. If these laws are violated, you give place to the devil and allow him to make you physically, mentally, and emotionally sick. If you don't believe and accept Jesus as your personal Savior, you cannot be born again and will continue to be at Satan's disposal. If you willfully walk in front of a moving train, you can expect to be injured. If you continually eat and drink the wrong things, your body cannot achieve or maintain health. You give the devil every right to afflict you, persecute you, cause you to lust, bring the cares of the world upon you, and produce deceit within you.

Poor eating habits may not appear to have any effect, but the results eventually catch up with you. After an extended time you become aware that you do not feel good. You walk into a doctor's office and say, "Cure me, Doc!" Or you go to a minister and say, "Pray that God will heal me now!"

God is gracious and does bring about healing, whether the manifestation is immediate or more gradual. One sure way to lose it, though, is to continue in bad habits. As one doctor stated, "You can either eat right, have good health, and live longer or eat junk, become sick, and die long before your time." The choice is yours.

As a believer you not only have been placed under a new rulership, but have also been given "*...all things that pertain unto life and godliness...*" *(II Peter 1:3)*, and blessed with "*...all spiritual blessings in heavenly places in Christ:*" *(Ephesians 1:3)* Satan has come to mar and destroy all things from God. That's just what he did in the beginning — when he attempted to destroy the paradise Adam and Eve enjoyed. He was trying to use man, God's ultimate creation, to strike back since he was unable to attack God directly.

But Satan is a defeated foe! The seed of woman (Jesus) has bruised his head. (Genesis 3:15) The rightful place of Satan is under your feet. You don't have to allow him to steal, kill, or destroy anything that the Word of God says is yours. You are told to resist him and he will flee from you. (James 4:7) Satan is to run from you — instead of you running from him.

AVENUES OF HEALING

There are generally two ways that you can receive your healing. Number one is through the help of others. Number two is by your own faith in believing, saying, and acting upon the Word of God. Let me show you a few of the ways by which you can receive your healing through the faith actions of other believers.

1) THE LAYING ON OF HANDS: The Bible calls the laying on of hands one of the foundation truths in the Christian life:

> *"Therefore leaving the principles of the doctrine of Christ, let us go on unto perfection; not laying again the foundation of repentance from dead works, and of faith toward God,*
> *V. 2, of the doctrine of baptisms, and of laying on of hands, and of resurrection of the dead, and of eternal judgment."* [Hebrews 6:1 & 2]

It is ironic to find the author of Hebrews urging Christians of his day to go beyond the elementary stage in their learning. Many people today have not even reached the knowledge of those things the book of Hebrews calls basic. For this reason I want to review the Bible teaching about the laying on of hands before offering instruction on how to receive your healing through this method.

The Word of God gives at least three basic reasons for the laying on of hands: as one means of receiving the Holy Ghost, as a means of receiving a spiritual gift, and as a means of receiving healing.

"And when Simon saw that through laying on

of the apostles' hands the Holy Ghost was given, he offered them money." [Acts 8:18]

"Neglect not the gift that is in thee, which was given thee by prophecy, with the laying on of the hands by the presbytery." [I Timothy 4:14]

"They shall take up serpents; and if they drink any deadly thing, it shall not hurt them; they shall lay hands on the sick, and they shall recover." [Mark 16:18]

The laying on of hands imparts spiritual power to the recipient. The power is not in the hands of the person who uses this method, but in the Spirit of God. The laying on of hands can be done by **any** believer. I have heard protests from those using Acts 8:18, which says that the apostles laid their hands on people. They say that it occured then, but they've been gone almost 2,000 years. I can prove to you from the Word of God, though, that it was not just the apostles who laid hands on people.

Acts 9 tells of a certain disciple, Ananias, who laid hands on Paul for him to receive his sight and be filled with the Holy Ghost. Acts 13 lists the names of certain prophets and teachers in the church in Antioch, none of whom were apostles. When the Holy Spirit told them to separate Paul and Barnabus for God's work, they fasted, prayed, and laid their hands on them. So you can see that the apostles were not the only ones used in the laying on of hands.

The laying on of hands should be practiced by all believers. Jesus Himself laid hands on people — and He is your example. Luke 13 tells how Jesus laid hands on the woman bound with the spirit of infirmity for 18 years, and she was immediately made straight. Jesus laid hands on the blind man of Bethsaida, but the man received only a partial healing at first. Mark 8:23-25 says:

> *"And he took the blind man by the hand, and led him out of the town; and when he had spit on his eyes, and put his hands upon him, he asked him if he saw ought.*
> *V. 24, And he looked up, and said, I see men as trees, walking.*
> *V. 25, After that he put his hands again upon his eyes, and made him look up: and he was restored, and saw every man clearly."*

Notice that the account doesn't say Jesus prayed twice to ask God to heal the man. It says that He laid His hands on him twice.

Mark gives an account of one of the rulers of the synagogue, Jairus, who came and fell at Jesus' feet, begging Him to come and lay hands on his dying daughter. Jesus was delayed by the throngs of people and found the girl dead when he arrived. The Bible says that Jesus took her by the hand and told her to arise — **and she did!** Oh, the power of the laying on of hands!

You can lay your hands on the sick, and they will recover (if you believe the Word of God). Too many people are afraid of what others will think of them. They worry that someone may see them and think that they are a fanatic. Don't be concerned that someone may see you. The only way that an unbeliever can see the sign of the wonders of God is if you openly work the works of God. Someone, although they may be skeptical and mocking at first, can do nothing but marvel at a miracle.

I have no embarrassment when it comes to following the Bible. Some people say, "That's not dignified." My answer to them is what I once heard Brother John Osteen say, "The most dignified people in the world are in a cemetary!" Since I heard that, I quit trying to be dignified.

There is a rather humorous account in the Old Testament about the laying on of hands. Job told his friend, *"Lay your hand upon your mouth." (Job 21:5)* If there was more laying of hands on individuals' mouths to keep from speaking sickness into existence ("I'm afraid I'm catching a cold," etc.), there would be less need for the laying on of hands to obtain healing. Doesn't God have a beautiful sense of humor? You need to say what Charles Capps said one day when he started sneezing: "I believe I'm coming down with a healing."

If you are sick, even as you read this chapter, believe that the laying on of hands is one method God uses to heal people. Call on someone you know is a believer and get him/her to lay hands on you. The Bible says that with the laying on of hands, people shall recover. If you are well, you can have the power to lay hands on the sick yourself. Start laying hands on other people. You might say, "But, I've never done that before." That doesn't matter. When the Bible says it, you are to do it. If you do, you will start seeing results!

2) GIFTS OF THE SPIRIT

Paul wrote to the church at Corinth:

> *"Now concerning spiritual gifts, brethren, I would not have you ignorant.*
> *V. 4, Now there are diversities of gifts, but the same Spirit.*
> *V. 7, But the manifestation of the Spirit is given to every man to profit withal.*
> *V. 8, For to one is given by the Spirit the word of wisdom; to another the word of knowledge by the same Spirit;*
> *V. 9, To another faith by the same Spirit; to another the gifts of healing by the same Spirit;*
> *V. 10, To another the working of miracles; to another prophecy; to another discerning of spirits; to another divers kinds of tongues; to another interpretation of tongues:*
> *V. 11, But all these worketh that one and the selfsame Spirit, dividing to every man severally as he will. [I Corinthians 12:1,4,7-11]*

Healing may also come through the operation of one or more of the nine spiritual gifts that Paul listed. These gifts operate as the Spirit of God wills. You can't make these gifts work anytime you want to. If they are not triggered by the Spirit, they won't manifest. If I was able in my own power to make the gifts work, I would minister to everyone and see them healed instantly. I would like for the gifts of the Spirit to operate every time that I pray for someone, but they don't always do so.

Remember, there are many methods to obtain your healing from God. Don't wait for someone to come along with the gift of healing in operation. You might wait until you die. When you are prayed for and hands are laid on you, the work is done — you're healed. You may ask, "What if I still feel the pain?" Then you didn't receive a gift healing — an instantaneous miracle. But you got healed — regardless. This is where some people lose out. They run all over the creation seeking a gift healing.

Healing is in the Word, and "gift healing" is only one of the methods available to the believer. When I was travelling as an evangelist, I often saw the same people in the prayer line at every crusade. They were going from meeting to meeting, seeking a gift healing. They'd go to one evangelist and get in his prayer line, then to another evangelist, then another. Because they didn't get a gift healing, they thought they hadn't been healed.

The gifts are in action as the Spirit chooses to employ them. Don't seek only a gift healing. If you still hurt, go home and say, "I am healed by the stripes of Jesus."

Some people ask, "Isn't it kind of foolish to say that if you still hurt?" There are two kinds of truth: sense knowledge truth (what you know through your five senses) and and revelation truth (what the Word reveals). I'm not suggesting that you say you're not hurting when you hurt. But I am telling you to confess that you're healed by the stripes of Jesus Christ. If you believe the Word of God **more** than you believe the symptoms, the symptoms will go!

3) ANOINTING WITH OIL

Another method of receiving your healing is by anointing with oil. James gives the following instructions:

> *"Is any sick among you? let him call for the elders of the church; and let them pray over him, anointing him with oil in the name of the Lord:*
> *V. 15, And the prayer of faith shall save the sick, and the Lord shall raise him up; and if he have committed sins, they shall be forgiven him.*
> *V. 16, Confess your faults one to another, and pray one for another, that ye may be healed. The effectual fervent prayer of a righteous man availeth much." [James 5:14-16]*

This method is specifically designed for someone who is sick at home, unable to attend a healing service, or to believe for themselves. For it to be effective, it is important that the elders be full of the Holy Ghost and faith in God. One time I was asked to go with some church elders to pray for a lady who was severely ill. When we got to her home, one of the elders said, "She's too bad to believe God for."

That was nonsense. He was looking at the circumstances and believing in her condition more than he was believing the Bible. When I pray for somebody, it doesn't matter what shape they are in. I don't look at that. I believe what the Word says. When you come to me for prayer, it doesn't matter what you need in the physical realm. God's Word says that it has already been done. The price has already been paid through Jesus Christ. I believe that more than I believe anything else.

Don't call for the kind of elders who say, "Lord, if it be Thy will, heal So-and-So." It is God's will to heal **every** Christian. Matthew 8:17 says that Jesus bore your sicknesses, and if He has borne them for you, why do you have to bear them? You don't — and there is something wrong if you do.

4) PRAYER OF AGREEMENT

"Again I say unto you, That if two of you shall agree on earth as touching anything that they shall ask, it shall be done for them of my Father which is in heaven.

V. 20, For where two or three are gathered together in my name, there am I in the midst of them." [Matthew 18:19 & 20]

While these words of Jesus don't specifically mention healing, they do promise that the Father will grant **anything that they ask**. The word agree here means "to be harmonious, to be suitable, to stipulate and be specific as in the terms of a contract."

People praying together have to know what they are praying about to be effective and get results. So often people want me to agree with them about "unspoken requests." How can you be in harmony and stipulate a desired result for a request that is unspoken? How can I be in harmony with you if I don't know what I am harmonizing about?

One time in Florida a lady came to me and said, "I've got a request; will you agree with me?" I asked her what it was. She said, "Well, I'd rather not tell you." I told her that if it was personal, she could go to my wife and let her pray the prayer of agreement. She said that it wasn't really that personal. I asked her again what it was. I was trying to let her know that I couldn't pray unless I knew what I was praying about.

She finally told me that she had been married 6 times and now had her eyes on another handsome fellow. "Would you pray that he'll fall in love with me, and we'll get married?" she asked. I told her that I wouldn't. She didn't think I'd agree with her about it if I knew the situation, and that was why she told me she had an unspoken request. You must know what you are agreeing with someone about.

The prayer of agreement between husband and wife is one of, if not the most powerful tool at the disposal of a family. Let me share an experience that we had with our daughter, Tammy, that took the power of two people agreeing.

TAMMY'S STORY

It was late that afternoon in October of 1969, about 5:30. I was sitting in a restaurant in Fort Worth, Texas. A voice came over the loudspeaker saying,

"Emergency phone call for Don Clowers!" I got up quickly, wondering what it could be. On the other end of the line was my wife, Sharon, with a sense of urgency in her voice. She told me that our 6-year-old daughter, Tammy, had been struck by an automobile. The injuries were very severe, and the doctor had no expectation of her living until I could get there.

I was an evangelist and away from home much of the time. As a result, Sharon was accustomed to handling any situation that arose. This time, however, was different. She said, "Honey, it's so bad. You must come home."

I felt so weak that I could hardly stand. I rushed out of the restaurant to my room in the hotel and called the airlines for the earliest flight back to my home, Chattanooga, Tennessee. I explained the urgency of my need and hung up the phone. As I was waiting for the agency to call me back, I began to pray. As well as I was able, I controlled my emotions and began to speak over Tammy all the scriptures that I knew concerning healing. With all the faith that I had, I asked God to let Tammy live and give my wife and me strength to stand.

In a few minutes the airline agent called me back with a time and flight number. While in the air I continued to confess God's Word and believe that He was healing Tammy at that very moment.

I arrived at the hospital at 2:30 the following morning. When I found Sharon, she was in a state of shock. As I got to Tammy's bed, I was not prepared for what I saw. It was almost more than I could bear. They told me that she had a severe concussion with brain damage, damaged kidneys, a broken leg, and multiple abrasions.

The doctor told us that he had no hope at all for her. He said that if she did happen to live, though, she would be totally unresponsive, a "vegetable," for the rest of her life. Sharon and I took hands according to Matthew 18:19, prayed the prayer of agreement, and sought every way that we knew to grasp hope. We made the effort to consider the Word of God, not the condition of Tammy's body.

At 5 o'clock one of my dearest friends came by and told me that he had prayed about Tammy. He said that God had told him Tammy was going to die. I neither wanted nor needed to hear those words. I was needing someone to come and stand with Sharon and me; someone who would say about Tammy what David said of himself: "*I shall live and declare the works of God.*"

After my friend spoke, something rose up inside me, and I said, "Lord, Your Word says that Tammy was healed by the stripes of Jesus!" When I made that statement, I knew we had a decision to make. It was either to rely on God's Word or give up and let nature take its course. There and then Sharon and I chose to believe God rather than what the devil would have us believe. We totally trusted God to be glorified in this situation.

For ten days Tammy clung to life in the Intensive Care Unit. There was no change in her physical condition, but we kept our faith and hope in God. At 6:30 in the morning on the 11th day, the doctor called me outside from the waiting room. He told me again that there had been no change; she was still in a coma, and he thought she could die at any time.

I thanked him for his kindness and honesty then told him that I believed God was healing Tammy completely. He looked at me as if to say: "You've lost touch with reality. You're seeking something that is impossible." I paid no attention to his expression and went back into the waiting room where 20 or so people were sitting. I began to sing a song of praise to the Lord.

GLIMMER OF HOPE

In just a few minutes a nurse came in almost shouting, "Mr. Clowers, come quickly!" She spoke with so much enthusiasm that I knew the news was going to be good. I hurried to Tammy's room and as I got to the side of her bed, Tammy began to blink her eyes. Although she did not respond when I spoke to her, I took her blinking as the first step to recovery. I ran out of the room to the nurse's station exclaiming, "Tammy is blinking her eyes! Tammy is blinking her eyes!" I called many of my friends, both local and long distance, to give them the good report.

Tammy continued to show small signs of improvement. The doctor gave us frequent reports on her progress, reports of things she could do that he felt she could have never attained in a comatose state.

After five weeks Tammy was moved from Intensive Care to Special Care. I took that as a positive move. Our families were supportive, but there were those who would give us no hope. One look at Tammy and they would say that she just couldn't live and be normal again. She lay there, seemingly unable to move any part of her body except her eyelids.

To Sharon and me, though, every day was one day closer to wholeness. We had prayed the prayer of agreement and believed that it worked. The IV was removed, and a nasal tube was placed for feeding purposes. Tammy's eyes began to follow people as they would enter or leave the room, but she showed no emotion.

After two months I asked if I could take Tammy home and was permitted to do so. At first she displayed no coordination whatsoever. She could not sit up and did not seem to relate to anything that was going on around her. Nevertheless, I would stand over her bed and pray, thanking God for the sound and healthy girl that I knew as my daughter.

After being home three days, a miraculous thing occurred. I was in Tammy's room strumming on a guitar and singing to her about how curly her hair was, how beautiful her brown eyes were. This was a tune of what I wanted her to be, not what was before my eyes. As I was singing to her, I looked and saw a little tear run down her face. I knew then that I had been communicating with her and that she was able to communicate with me once more.

A few weeks later I had come in very late from a long meeting and was resting for most of the day.

Sharon had taken Tammy from her bed and laid her on the den couch to watch television. A comedy was on at the time, and something very funny happened. Tammy suddenly laughed out loud. I instantly came awake at the sound of her voice and ran into the room. Sharon asked her to say, "Mamma," and she did. I asked her to say, "Daddy." When she said it, Sharon and I truly knew that "joy unspeakable and full of glory."

From that day forward she made regular steps to total recovery. Tammy has since graduated from high school and works a full time position at our church. Fellow believers, the prayer of agreement works!

5) SPECIAL MIRACLES

One of the most interesting ways that you can receive healing through the help of another is what the Bible calls special miracles. This kind of healing is something out of the ordinary, something that doesn't happen all of the time.

> *V. 11, "And God wrought special miracles by the hands of Paul:*
> *V. 12, So that from his body were brought unto the sick handkerchiefs or aprons, and the diseases departed from them, and the evil spirits went out of them." [Acts 19:11 & 12]*

You must understand that the handkerchiefs referred to in this passage had no power in themselves. They were anointed by Paul, and it was the faith of the people which caused the miracle-working power of God to come forth. I have sent out anointed prayer cloths for many years and have had wonderful reports of how God has moved in the lives of the people. Not long ago, a testimonial letter came to my office, and I'd like to share part of it with you.

Dear Brother and Sister Clowers,

I need prayer for my left side. It is giving me trouble. Please send me an anointed cloth. I know Jesus will heal me because you prayed for me about five years ago, and God healed my jaw. It was broken and the X-rays showed it. The doctor wanted to cut my jaw open and take out pieces of bone. He said he didn't know whether it would get well or not. But I wrote you to send me a prayer cloth. I thank Jesus, because when you prayed, Jesus healed my broken jaw. My jaw is well.

This is just one report from a person who received a special miracle, and many other reports could be given. Healing can be yours, though — even without the help of others — through your own faith.

YOU CAN BE HEALED THROUGH YOUR OWN FAITH

I want to share with you one of the most powerful methods by which you can receive healing. It is dependent upon no one else — you can utilitze this system entirely on your own.

> *"And Jesus answering saith unto them, Have faith in God.*
> *V. 23, For verily I say unto you, That whosoever shall say unto this mountain, Be thou removed, and be thou cast into the sea; and shall not doubt in his heart, but shall*

believe that those things which he saith shall come to pass; he shall have whatsoever he saith.

V. 24, Therefore I say unto you, What things soever ye desire, when ye pray, believe that ye receive them, and ye shall have them." [Mark 11:22-24]

This powerful passage reveals that you can receive healing through your own faith in a process of saying, believing, and receiving. Before ***delving*** into this process, look again at Mark 11:23:

"For verily I say unto you, That whosoever shall say unto this mountain, Be thou removed, and be thou cast into the sea; and shall not doubt in his heart, but shall believe that those things which he saith shall come to pass; he shall have whatsoever he ***saith."***

This verse of scripture can work to your benefit or your detriment, depending on how you choose to use it. I firmly believe that words have power. Few realize the influence exerted with words and consider what escapes through the mouth. The Bible clearly states, *"Death and life are in the power of the tongue,..." (Proverbs 18:21)* You have the authority to speak words of life or death, whichever you choose. Jesus stated in Mark 11 how to use the power of words to destroy any obstacle. He said that you must say to the mountain, "Be removed!"

At one time or another everyone faces a mountainous problem or a seemingly impossible situation. Jesus said that the way to remove it is to take the

Word of God which has been planted, speak to the problem, and begin to positively confess the fulfillment of the need.

The word **confess** holds various meanings for different people. When I say **confess**, I am not talking of admitting how many problems there are or how impossible a situation seems. When I am faced with danger, I begin to confess that I am God's child, that I am an overcomer, and that I do not have fear. Before sickness threatens my family or me, I begin to confess that Jesus paid for our healing at Calvary and that we are well and healthy. I believe it in my heart and confess it with my mouth.

I can already hear some people saying, "But what about the symptoms? If I confess that I am well, and I still hurt, what then?" No one can deny that the symptoms are there. Confessing that symptoms are not there when it is obvious that they are is truly a lie. They exist, but by believing the Word of God and confessing that belief, you take away their right to exist.

When their right to exist is removed, they have no choice but to leave. Why?

> *"While we look not at the things which are seen, but at the things which are not seen: for the things which are seen are temporal; but the things which are not seen are eternal." (II Corinthians 4:18]*

The spirit world called the natural world into existence and is in authority over it. Jesus also said, *"My Words, they are Spirit and they are life."* The result of this is that when you speak the words of Jesus, your words become spirit and prevail over anything natural. Instead of confessing symptoms, draw the Word of God out of your spirit and say, "I believe that I am healed by the stripes of Jesus."

Satan will attack and try to steal the seeds which have been planted by causing you to look at the symptoms instead of the Word. You must stand strong on your confession, though, until the visual image which you have of yourself aligns with the Word of God. Romans 4:17 says that you are "*to call those things which be not as though they were.*"

Throughout the many years I have been in the ministry, I have literally seen hundreds of people who believe that God chastens and teaches them through ill health and adverse situations in their lives. From His Word, though, you can see that God loves you and has provided health for you. In Acts 5:16, sick people were brought to the apostles. The Bible says that everyone was healed. There's no indication whatsoever that some of the people were not healed, because they were being chastened.

> "*There came also a multitude out of the cities round about into Jerusalem, bringing sick folks, and them which were vexed with unclean spirits: and they were healed every one.*"

They brought people who were sick and diseased and laid them on couches and beds in the streets. Everyone came, because they heard the call of healing and of the miracles being performed. The scripture does not indicate in any way whatsoever that there were some who could not be healed or were turned away, because they were being chastened or disciplined.

If sickness is a discipline why do people go to doctors and take medication for relief? It appears to me that if a person believes that sickness and disease is the chastening of the Lord, he is wrong by going to a doctor.

James 5:14 says, ***"If there are any sick among you..."*** Why didn't the Bible say, "You who are not being chastened let him call?" ***"Let him call"*** is a command. Therefore, to teach that sickness and disease are used by the Father to chasten would lead to a violation of the commission which James gave. Furthermore, a person would be afraid to call for fear of interfering with God's chastening. What would it accomplish for the elders to pray for him until the chastening was over? When the time came, God would withdraw the chastening automatically, as would any good Father, and there would be no need to bother the elders of the church.

> *"When his disciples James and John saw this, they said, Lord, wilt thou that we command fire to come down from heaven, and consume them, even as Elias did?*
> *V. 55, But he turned, and rebuked them, and said, Ye know not what manner of spirit ye are of.*
> *V. 56, For the Son of man is not come to*

destroy men's lives, but to save them. And they went to another village." [Luke 9:54-56]

This is a perfect example of Jesus Himself saying that He came to save men's lives. He had not been received, but he had compassion. I have pointed out that John 10:10 says, *"The thief cometh not, but for to steal, and to kill, and to destroy."* Jesus would be working against Himself if He destroyed lives. The disciples wanted to call fire down from heaven and destroy the men, but Jesus told them that He had come to save men.

There are also those who believe that God uses the devil to chasten. Does a good father take care of his own or does he call his enemy? Can you imagine God calling the devil and saying, "Satan, one of my children is getting out of hand. I'm giving you permission to give him a disease to correct him." And can't you hear the devil say, "Sure God, I'll do that. I wouldn't want to see him backslide and go to hell, so I'm going to put a sickness or disease on him. It will teach him something, and he'll get back with you." God doesn't need any help from the devil. Satan is God's enemy. He is not going to help you in training, but he will hinder you in any way that he can.

I want you to understand that God is a God of love, and He trains and teaches through His Word. You don't have to take either training or teaching if you don't want to. There are some people who don't want to be taught of the Lord. The Word of God goes forth, God teaches and instructs through His Word, but they refuse to hear, listen to, or believe it. The result is self destruction.

> *"If ye endure chastening, God dealeth with you as sons; for what son is he whom the father chasteneth not? But if he be without chastisement, whereof all are partakers, then are ye bastards, and not sons." [Hebrews 12:7]*

Several years ago a man came into my office and began to share with me how he had lost his business. At the time that he saw me he was working for someone else and making a menial salary. He believed that God had taken his business away from him. He said that when he first went into business, he was going to church and paying his tithes. As the business prospered, he began to put more time into the business and quit tithing. He said that as a result, God had to get his attention by taking his business. He related to me that he had returned to church and was living close to God. He also stated that he was satisfied with the menial amount of money that he was receiving.

I told him that God did not take his business. He reaped from the seed which he had sown. When he asked me what I meant, I replied, "You said, yourself, that you were going to church and tithing. Your business became prosperous. After it prospered, you began staying out of church and quit tithing. You began sowing bad seeds, your business went sour, and you lost everything that you had. You called out to God when you were on the very bottom. If you had remained faithful, your business would have continued to grow, and you would have had more money to give into the kingdom of God."

You see, that was nothing but a lie of the devil for this man to have only a meager income after he was finally straightened out. He is now very limited to what he can give to God. God wants you to be prosperous so that you will have thousands of dollars to give into the gospel.

WHAT ABOUT JOB?

Someone inevitably asks the question, "Well, what about Job? God took away from him." God **did not** take away from Job. If you will read in the book of Job, you will begin to understand some things as I have. Job said, "*the Lord giveth and the Lord taketh away...*" Job was unable to obtain understanding from a Bible such as you have today. He had an incomplete revelation of God and very little idea that there was even a devil. In fact, many people in the Old Testament had little revelation of the devil. If they had been given revelation of Satan, they would have actively served him as god of the earth.

You may have heard the expression, "I guess I'm just like old Job; God's just testing me." No! God is not testing and trying you. James 1:13 & 14 states,

> *V. 13, "Let no man say when he is tempted, I am tempted of God: for God cannot be tempted with evil, neither tempteth he any man:*
> *V. 14, But every man is tempted, when is drawn away of his own lust and enticed."*

God would not test you to see how much faith you have. He knows how much faith you have. He knows you better than you know yourself. Tests and trials come to destroy your faith.

> "*...Affliction or persecution ariseth for the word's sake...*" *[Mark 4:17]*

The afflictions and persecutions of this life come to steal the Word of God from you or to stop you from operating on the amount of Word that you have inside. Faith without actions is dead. (James 2:20) God is not trying to destroy your faith — He is trying to help you succeed!

Before I go into detail concerning Job, I want to remind you again that in the Old Testament people did not have complete revelation of Satan and his work as is available today. They did not have the light of the New Testament. Therefore, many times, they attributed situations to God that were really from the enemy.

I want to answer the question, "Did God afflict Job?" The answer is "No!" Look at what the Word of God says about it:

> "***For the thing which I greatly feared is come upon me, and that which I was afraid of is come unto me.***" ***[Job 3:25]***
>
> "***And the Lord said unto Satan, Behold, all that he has is in thy power; only upon himself put not forth thine hand...***" ***[Job 1:12]***

Job had placed himself in the hand of the enemy through fear. Satan tried to persuade God to curse Job, and God wouldn't do it. (Job 1:10-11) God said, "*Behold (or Look), all that he has is in your power.*" Fear opened the door for Satan to come in and kill, steal, and destroy Job. Ephesians 4:27 says, "*Neither give place to the devil.*"

In I John 4:18, God gives the mark of perfection in the New Covenant — "*Perfect love casteth out fear.*" In the New Covenant you have knowledge of the fact that Jesus already suffered for you. Job neither had the knowledge nor was expected to have it. God called him perfect and upright even though he had fear.

Did Job know the source of his trouble? He really didn't, because he said in Job 10:15, "*I am full of confusion.*" In Job 9:17 he thought God was breaking him with a tempest...'*For he breaketh me with a tempest, and multiplieth my wounds without cause.*" Then in Job 6:4, "*For the arrows of the Almighty are within me, the poison whereof drinketh up my spirit: the terrors of God do set themselves in array against me.*" Job thought God had destroyed him. In Job 16:11, Job thought God had turned him over to the hands of the wicked.

In Job 42:3, he admitted that he did not understand: "*Therefore have I uttered that I understood not.*" In his confusion, Job thought he was being refined — "*...When he hath tried me, I shall come forth as gold.*" *(Job 23:10) Satan tried to get Job to curse God. Job said,* "*All that man hath will he give for his life.*" God had already declared that Job was perfect and upright. Therefore, he was not being refined. God does not use Satan to act as the refiner of **His children.** If he is refining God's people, then he is working against himself.

Look at what Job said when the servant came to tell him about the calamities that had taken place and about the death of his children.

> "...*Naked came I out of my mother's womb, and naked shall I return thither; the Lord gave and the Lord hath taken away: blessed be the name of the Lord.*" *[Job 1:21]*

It is true that Job made this statement — but, it is not a statement of truth. Job thought that God had destroyed his possessions and his children. I have already showed you that God told Satan, "*all that he has is in **your** power.*" I have heard ministers who were ignorant of the truth of God's Word use this scripture in funerals where tragedy has struck a home. God is the author of life. God is the author of good gifts for His children — not heartache, pain, and sorrow.

> "*And the Lord turned the captivity of Job, when he prayed for his friends; also the Lord gave Job twice as much as he had before.*" *[Job 42:10]*

God turned the captivity of Job around. Who had he been in captivity to? It was Satan. Fear has torment and holds people in bondage. His fear brought him into captivity by Satan, but, Praise the Lord, God is bigger than any fear. He is bigger than any problem or mountain that you face. God also blessed Job with much more than he had in the beginning.

> "*So the Lord blessed the latter end of Job more*

than the beginning:..."
V. 16, After this Job lived an hundred and forty years, and saw his sons, and his sons' sons, even four generations." [Job 42:12 & 16]

Many people assume that the period of distress in Job's life lasted for years. Hebrew Scholars have concluded that the calamities described in Job took place over not longer than a 9 month period. You see, the end of the story is not one of defeat and failure. It is one of victory with the blessings of God overtaking Job. He lived 140 more years in prosperity! If you are just an "old Job," then shout the praises of God. Your deliverance is coming. Victory is on the way. You'll be blessed far greater in your latter days than you were in your former days. Get ready to be blessed by God and see the enemy's plans defeated.

PAUL'S THORN

"And lest I should be exalted above measure through the abundance of revelations, there was given to me a thorn in the flesh, the messenger of Satan to buffet me, lest I should be exalted above measure."
V. 8, For this thing I besought the Lord thrice, that it might depart from me.
V. 9, And he said unto me, My grace is sufficient for thee: for my strength is made perfect in weakness. Most gladly therefore will I rather glory in my infirmities, that the power of Christ may rest upon me.

> *V. 10, Therefore I take pleasure in infirmities, in reproaches, in necessities, in persecutions, in distresses for Christ's sake: for when I am weak, then am I strong." [II Corinthians 12:7-10]*

Paul said, "*there was given to me a thorn in the flesh.*" Paul didn't say God was the one responsible for it. Many people think that God gave it to him, but that is not true. Some authorities believe that the thorn was a physical sickness. I want to show you some other scriptures which refer to thorns and see if they refer to sickness.

> "*Speak unto the children of Israel, and say unto them, When ye are passed over Jordan into the land of Canaan;*
> *V. 52, Then ye shall drive out all the inhabitants of the land from before you, and destroy all their pictures, and destroy all their molten images, and quite pluck down all their high places:*
> *V. 53, And ye shall dispossess the inhabitants of the land, and dwell therein: for I have given you the land to possess it.*
> *V. 54, And ye shall divide the land by lot for an inheritance among your families, and to the more ye shall give the more inheritance, and to the fewer ye shall give the less inheritance: every man's inheritance shall be in the place where his lot falleth; according to the tribes of your fathers ye shall inherit.*
> *V. 55, But if ye will not drive out the in-*

habitants of the land from before you; then it shall come to pass, that those which ye let remain of them shall be pricks in your eyes, and thorns in your sides, and shall vex you in the land wherein ye dwell." [Numbers 33:51-55]

It is evident in the scriptures above that the word thorns is not speaking of sickness or disease. It is referring to people who are a nuisance or give you a hard time, those who would be a hindrance to you.

"But the sons of Belial shall be all of them as thorns thrust away, because they cannot be taken with hands:" [II Samuel 23:6]

In this verse David is saying that the sons of Belial (who represent Satan) will be as a thorn thrust away. Thorn is not referring to sickness in this passage.

Paul even goes on to describe what the thorn is in II Corinthians 12:7, he states, "*...a thorn in the flesh, the messenger of Satan to buffet me...*" The Greek word for messenger is Angelos. We get the English word **angel** from it. In other words, there was a personal demon assigned to harass and buffet Paul. That was his thorn in the flesh. You can quickly see that this demon did a good job in giving Paul a lot of trouble. Paul suffered shipwreck, beatings, and was thrown into prison.

He said in verse 8 that he prayed 3 times for the Lord to remove this hindrance. God's answer to him was:

"And he said unto me, My grace is sufficient for thee: for my strength is made perfect in

weakness..." [II Corinthians 12:9]

What was God saying? He was not saying for Paul to just put up with it. God said, ***"My grace is sufficient."*** The word **grace** here means benefit, favor, and gift. Sufficient, according to Strong's Concordance, means "to avail, to ward off." God said, "*My gift, benefit, and favor will prevail. My grace and benefits are powerful enough to ward off the enemy. Rely on My grace, it is sufficient. When you are weak, then I am strong. Rely on My strength.*"

In other words, Paul had a right to use the name of Jesus and God's power would prevail. God's grace is sufficient to meet every need — but you **must** exercise your right to use His name. God won't do it for you — you must speak His name for yourself.

THE MAN BORN BLIND

"And as Jesus passed by, he saw a man which was blind from his birth.
V. 2, And his disciples asked him, saying, Master, who did sin, this man, or his parents, that he was born blind.
V. 3, Jesus answered, Neither hath this man sinned, nor his parents: but that the works of God should be made manifest in him.
V. 4, I must work the works of him that sent me, while it is day: the night cometh, when no man can work.
V. 5, As long as I am in the world, I am the light of the world.

> *V. 6, When he had thus spoken, he spat on the ground, and made clay of the spittle, and he anointed the eyes of the blind man with the clay,*
> *V. 7, And said unto him, Go wash in the pool of Siloam (which is by interpretation, Sent). He went his way therefore, and washed, and came seeing."* *[John 9:1-7]*

The scriptures above give many people problems. At the surface it appears that God made him blind so that Jesus could heal him — but that is not what the scripture says.

Jesus and his disciples were passing and saw a blind man. The disciples asked Jesus the question, "Who sinned to cause this man to be born blind? Was it him or his parents?" I heard one man say, "If it was his own sin, he must have been a mean, little rascal while he was in his mother's womb." Jesus answered them and said, *"It was not the sin of this man, nor the sin of his parents that caused him to be born blind."*

Look at Jesus' next remarks **very closely.**

> *"Jesus answered, Neither hath this man sinned, nor his parents: but that the works of God should be made manifest in him.*
> *V. 4, I must work the works of him that sent me, while it is day: the night cometh, when no man can work."* *[John 9:3 & 4]*

Jesus then proceeded to do the works of God and heal the blind man. Jesus said He was the "**light of the world.**" He let that light within Him shine out to dispel the force of darkness upon those around him.

You see, my friend, healing brings glory to God. It magnifies His name. It shows us that His power is still active today. Reach out and receive it.

Chapter 5

DESIRE

Do you desire God's best for your life or are you satisfied with mediocracy? Some people say, "I am happy and content just being average." I heard one person give a definition of average as being "the best of the worst, or the worst of the best." That does not sound like God to me. God's desire is for you to be the best of the best and prosper in everything that you do. Why accept anything less?

In Matthew 6, Jesus was teaching His disciples how to pray. One particular part of this prayer stands out to me. He said, *"Thy will be done in earth as it is in Heaven."* How are things in heaven? I know your answer already. Of course, you said, "Great!" What is He calling the earth, though? Is it the trees, stones, dirt, or grass? No, **you** are the earth. He is saying that He desires for you to have what He has.

YOUR DESIRE SHOULD BE GOD'S DESIRE

Some people say, "I would be satisfied with just getting by. I really don't need that **extra** bedroom, a better car, or nice clothes." But friends, why live with **less** when God has already provided **more** for you? I believe that there are as many people who never achieve or have better things in life because of a lack of desire as those who never achieve because of doubt and unbelief.

DESIRE THE BEST

"Therefore I say unto you, What things soever

ye desire, when ye pray, believe that ye receive them, and ye shall have them." [Mark 11:24]

Jesus said "**you**" five times in this verse of scripture. God is concerned about **you** and **your desires** as much as He is concerned about **your needs.** Think about this...when He gives you the desires of your heart, the needs of others *will be* met. Begin to think in agreement with the Word and don't let anyone else condemn you. **Don't condemn yourself** either because of a desire for better things in life.

DESIRE IS SCRIPTURAL

I know that people will say, "God has promised to supply my needs but not my desires." Let's look at another scripture besides Mark 11:24 to see what the Bible says about desires. *"Delight thyself also in the Lord; and he shall give thee the desires of thine heart." [Psalm 37:4]*

The word desire comes from a Hebrew word **MISHALAH** which means "a request, desire, or petition." The word request according to Webster means "the act of asking or expressing a desire." So when you delight yourself in the Lord according to Psalm 37:4 and Mark 11:24, whatever you desire, request, or petition, the Lord will give it to you. He will give you **all things.**

ALL THINGS ARE YOURS

"According as his divine power hath given unto us all things that pertain unto life and

> *godliness, through the knowledge of him that hath called us to glory and virtue:*
> *V. 4, Whereby are given unto us exceeding great and precious promises: that by these ye might be partakers of the divine nature, having escaped the corruption that is in the world through lust." [II Peter 1:3 & 4]*

God has given you all things that pertain to life. Peter said that you are partakers of the Divine Nature, and God desires that you partake of the good things in life. There are many people in religious circles who have been taught that being a Christian is doing without, that you are humble when you have little material wealth. It attempts to make those who desire more in life feel guilty. **YOU ARE UNLIMITED!** Liberate yourself from all of the negative input that may have been taught to you. There is no reason why you should seek approval from others to have a successful, happy, and fulfilled life.

Don't wait for God's best until you get to heaven. You are alive unto God now. You are endowed with greatness now. You have the God-given ability to think, dream, talk, and do big things through Jesus Christ. You are God's ultimate — made in His image. Believe and meditate on this. Why would God want you to do without when He has plenty? He doesn't want you to live in lack. Feeling that you must is only what you have been told by men. You have escaped the corruption of the old man; you have laid him aside and taken Jesus as your Lord. Move up to God's level and don't make any excuses.

HE WILL GIVE YOU ALL THINGS

"But seek ye first the kingdom of God, and his righteousness; and all these things shall be added unto you." [Matthew 6:33]

"Jesus said unto him, If thou canst believe, all things are possible to him that believeth." [Mark 9:23]

"...how shall he not with him also freely give us all things?" [Romans 8:32]

GOOD THINGS

"If ye then, being evil, know how to give good gifts unto your children, how much more shall your Father which is in heaven give good things to them that ask him?" [Matthew 7:11]

ANYTHING YOU ASK

"If ye shall ask any thing in my name, I will do it." [John 14:14]

WHATSOEVER YOU ASK

"...that whatsoever ye ask of the Father in my name, he may give it you." [John 15:16]

"...Whatsoever ye shall ask the Father in my name, he will give it you." [John 16:23]

"And whatsoever we ask, we receive of him, because we keep his commandments, and do

those things that are pleasing in his sight." [I John 3:22]

"And this is the confidence that we have in him, that, if we ask any thing according to his will, he heareth us:

V. 15, And if we know that he hear us, whatsoever we ask, we know that we have the petitions that we desired of him." [I John 5:14 & 15]

ASK WHAT YOU WILL

"If ye abide in me, and my words abide in you, ye shall ask what ye will, and it shall be done unto you." [John 15:7]

MORE THAN YOU ASK

"Now to Him Who, by (in consequence of) the (action of His) power that is at work within us, is able to (carry out His purpose and) do superabundantly, far over and above all that we (dare) ask or think - infinitely beyond our highest prayers, desires, thoughts, hopes or dreams—" [Ephesians 3:20, Amplified]

After reading and meditating in these scriptures, you can see what God's Word says about you having the desires of your heart. The Word says that the power within you will give you far above and beyond your highest desires and dreams.

Many people are tolerating depleted, depressed, and deprived lives, simply because they have not been told the truth about God's Word. You can see however, what God has said. Consider His Word and look at the things that He wants to give you. Then you won't believe Satan's lies or put up with all the lack that you may have had in your life.

DO YOU ENJOY YOUR JOB?

Do you desire a better job? Do you enjoy working on the job that you already have? I was really surprised when I read some recent statistics showing how many people were unhappy with their jobs. As a child of God, you do not have to be unhappy or have a job that you don't enjoy. God's will is for you to do what you ***enjoy doing.*** First of all, though, you must be faithful where you are and do your best. God will promote you if you have desire and prove that you are willing to do and give your best.

I also read where 98% of the American workforce will not do their job unless they are directed and supervised. The statistics show that 84% of all employees demand constant direction and supervision. In other words, they are told exactly what to do and checked on constantly to see if they are doing it. This survey stated that 14% of all employees demand supervision **most** all of the time. This means that only 2% of the people will work unsupervised.

However, God's people are creative so this should not be true in the kingdom of God. A born-again child of God has been given wisdom in the New Birth, so he should be a self-starter, honest, and have the desire to succeed. With these qualities you can have what you want. You will change the statistics, because you take the power of God within you and obtain the things that you desire. The believer should be at the head and not on the bottom. You can own your own company or you can be the manager or supervisor of someone else's. Whatever you desire from God can be yours!

LIVE THE ABUNDANT LIFE

God places an extremely high value on the human being, because He paid such a great price to restore you to abundant life. As a result, it is **your** responsibility to make the choice to be free, succeed, and live a creative life with no more limitations. You have been created to live life as God lives it. The eagle was made to fly high and soar above the clouds and the fish to swim in the oceans of the world. Man was created with the desire to be like his Father God. It's right for the eagle to fly and the fish to swim. It's also right for you to be where God intended for you to be and do the things that He intended for you to do.

GOD'S BEST IS FOR ALL

"Which of you, if his son asks for bread, will give him a stone?
V. 10, or if he asks for a fish, will give him a snake?
V. 11, If you, then, though you are evil, know how to give good gifts to your children, how

much more will your Father in heaven give ***good gifts*** *to those that ask him!" [Matthew 7:9-11 NIV]*

Jesus said that a father desires to give good things to his son. How much more does your heavenly Father desire to give you good things!

It's not God's plan for only a small portion of the people in this world to have wealth. He has made it available for everyone. It is the one who desires it and will not compromise until he has attained his goal that will reach the top in this life. The born-again believers should be the ones controlling the wealth, and, in turn, ruling the world by enjoying **all** of God's treasures and using them to win the unreached with the Good News.

Many people have little or no encouragement from their spiritual leaders to reach for the top. Some go so far as to tell them that this is carnal and worldly. They quickly point out scriptures about lust and pride and show those in the Old Testament who failed because of greed. They preach guilt and say that seeking success is the wrong motive. This is a lie from Satan to keep the wealth from God's people and hinder the spreading of good news of the gospel. Satan does not care how religious you are as long as you do not learn to be the person God desires for you to be and reach the level of success to further the work of God. If there is anyone around you who tells you not to seek the better things of God because you are unworthy, just go back and read the chapter on your righteousness. Then you will wake up, step up, and live up to the good things in life for you.

POSSESS GOOD THINGS

Remind yourself each day that the world is not here to consume you by its negative environments. You have been given God's ability to possess the good things in this life. You have a creative mind; and with God's power and your creative ideas and dreams, you can soar into the realms of the New Dimension. Never again allow circumstances or man to place you in a box, limit you, or cause you to accept less than your God-given desire.

DREAM BIG DREAMS

In 1981 Robert Tilton came to Chattanooga, Tennessee and spoke at my Campmeeting. Toward the end of the service he said to the congregation, "Turn around, shake hands with someone, and tell them that you're going to do what you have wanted to do and that you will take the first step before the week is out." There was a man there who had tried several small business ventures in addition to his regular job but had never given all of his effort to make them work. He had a good job and he and his wife were living comfortably. However, he desired to own his own business.

After hearing the statement that Bob had made, he turned around and made the confession as he had been asked to do. This was on a Tuesday evening. He put off what he had said that he would do until the last working day of the week. At the last moment he kept his word and went to another company and spoke to the owner about buying it. Even though he had very little cash at that time and only a moderate home, he had the desire and a dream to buy that business. Pastor Tilton had encouraged him to use his power to dream and get what he wanted. He was able to make a deal with the owner to buy the business. By natural standards, it was impossible, but he believed that it was God's will, that the desire was born from God.

When he purchased the company he did not know that the business was going downhill. He would come to church every service and hear the teaching from God's Word that he was unlimited and there was no mountain too big or no problem that he couldn't solve. He could do **all things** through Christ Jesus. Because he was new in the field and did not have a track record as the new owner, very few contracts were being signed. He held on to his desire and dream, though, worked diligently, and learned the business very quickly. The company's first year was a struggle and grossed only $400,000.00 in sales. He has been in the business 3 years, and as a result of standing fast in the Word, his company has grossed $4 million dollars this year alone, and there are several more months to go before his working year ends. This was accomplished because of a desire, the willingness to work, faith in God, and refusing any limitations that someone or circumstances would try to put before him.

SUCCESS IS YOURS

What would you dream if you believed it to be

possible? What would you believe if you knew that you would not fail? Any dream that God can put inside of you; if you believe it, with the power of God that is inside of you, you can have it. You must have a desire to have that dream. If mountains are between you and the fulfillment of that dream, you will not let them hinder you. You will instead move those mountains by the Word of God. Jesus said, "*Whosoever shall say unto this mountain, Be thou removed and cast into the sea; and shall not doubt, he shall have whatsoever he saith.*" This is your promise. Jesus is talking directly to you. Do you accept it as being for you?

GOD IS NO RESPECTOR OF PERSONS

Someone once said to me, "I believe the Bible, but I don't believe this success is for me. It may be for others, but I am not supposed to have these things." Now to me, this is a cop-out.

> "*Then Peter opened his mouth, and said, Of a truth I perceive that God is no respector of persons:*" *[Acts 10:34]*

Peter said that God is no respector of persons. However, if you allow the devil to tell you that you are not supposed to be given these things, then you will never have them.

Of course, there are those who say, "If I have all of the material things, I may not be very spiritual." Poor and humble do not go together even though man has done so. This has been a lie that Satan has told the body of Christ to keep them from reaching for a better life and having very little to support the gospel. It's also one of the lies that Satan has used to keep people from accepting Jesus Christ as Savior. They've been told that they have to give everything up to serve the Lord. God is the El Shaddai God, the God Who is more than enough. He has made all things for you. Don't be under condemnation because you desire them. As a child of God, you should have them.

PRAYER - MEDITATION - IMAGE

Dr. Paul Yonggi Cho, Pastor of the World's Largest Church, said, "Take the paintbrush of prayer and dip it into the ink of God's Word. Then write that picture or image on the canvas of your heart." This statement brings to mind something that I have spoken of before concerning the 100 fold return. I said that you must "see" your return before you are able to obtain it. The same applies to any desire, dream, or promise that God has for you.

There is more to "seeing" it than just writing down what you desire on a piece of paper and continually looking at it, although it is important to do so. You must picture the manifestation of the desire in your mind's eye, and a written goal reinforces this. If your pursuit stops there, though, you will not obtain the answer. Why? Because man is an emotional being, and emotions can be unstable, irrational, and misleading. If the confession (speaking the picture in your mind's eye) is as far as you go, you will find that there is no power in it to bring results. A storm will come, you will become discouraged, and probably say what many others in the same predicament say, "This faith stuff doesn't work."

The words, although sincere, are empty for lack of faith. Romans 10:17 says that faith comes by hearing and understanding the Word of God. This is more than just reading the Bible every day. The key to success is given in Dr. Cho's statement. Meditation in the Word and prayer, communication with your Father, brings the revelation (Rhema) of the Word that you are standing on from your spirit to your mind.

As you develop your faith by revelation on the Word through prayer, the power to change the situation or circumstance is added to the words that you speak (your confession). You begin to know that the desire which you have is your own and not someone else's. Only then can you pull out all stops and go full speed ahead. Any storm that Satan may bring will not discourage you, cause you to give up, or cause you to be defeated and retreat to something less than what you desire or dream. You stand in faith, not emotions.

SEIZE WITH A GRIP

"Therefore I say unto you, What things soever ye desire, when ye pray, believe that ye receive them, and ye shall have them." [Mark 11:24]

The word receive in the scripture above comes from the Greek word **LAMBANO**, which means "to take, to get hold of, seize." Jesus is saying to you that the responsibility lies in you taking hold of the answer, seizing it with your mind and body. It's already there, waiting to be brought from the spirit world, so you must be the one to bring it into the natural world.

Many times people desire and dream but will not take hold of that dream with a grip. As a result they tend to lose it before they see the **desired** results. I can't say it to you enough. **GOD HAS MORE THAN ENOUGH FOR YOU**, but you must be determined to hold to your answer with a grip so tight that you are unshakable from what you are expecting to take place in your life.

> *"Let them not depart from thine eyes; keep them in the midst of thine heart." [Proverbs 4:21]*

Keep the desire and dream in front of you at all times. Write it down. As I said before, it is important to **write** down exactly what you desire. The vision must be where you can see it at home and at work. Solomon said to keep the Word in front of you and in your heart. The Word brings your desire to pass as you meditate, pray, and become a doer of It, so don't let a day go by without looking at your desire and dream. As you do these things, the answer moves little-by-little from the spirit realm into the natural realm.

PUSH FORWARD - BREAK OUT - GO OVER

Think on this for a moment. It would be great to give more to God this year, more the next year, and even more the next. Yes, this should be the normal. Staying at the same level of giving tithes and offering or going backwards is not living up to your full potential. Now I'm not condemning, just reminding you again not to let Satan steal from you. Don't become complacent and satisfied with giving just a few dollars a week. **PUSH FORWARD, BREAK OUT, AND GO OVER!** Do more than you have ever done. Help others who are hurting. Don't let your life be one of continual struggle. God isn't struggling; why should you? You should be able to wear the kind of clothes, drive the kind of car, have the kind of furniture, and live in the kind of house that you desire.

Consider again what heaven is like. If you've done any studying at all, you know how beautiful it must be there. Luke 11:2 says, "*...Thy will be done, as in heaven, so in earth.*" You are the earth and God is saying to you, "I want you to have good things here and now." It is not His will for you to be deprived until you get to heaven. Set your heart and eyes on God's lifestyle. Once you have begun to taste of it, you will never let man or circumstances keep you from it. Even when tests and trials come, you'll never bow or back up but will see that the attack is from Satan; and that this should not be an excuse to give up, but an opportunity to receive from God. Instead of being crushed by the problem, you will dream bigger dreams, take bigger steps, do more than you have ever done, and have more of God's blessings upon you. Once you are enlightened to God's will, you will never retreat to the old things of yesterday. You already know what God wants for you. Set your face in that direction, not the problem. It is only temporary. God's Word is true and everlasting.

His Word is the prevailing force that changes those things around you.

Be prepared to stand for a while if necessary. My wife and I had some desires and dreams. We knew that we had them, but it took almost 6 years for some of them to be brought from the spirit realm into the natural realm. Nevertheless, believe me, they were worth waiting for. Two years before we began to see the manifestation of our desires and dreams begin to unfold, Satan sent a storm to cause us to give up and get our eyes on something else. We kept on standing, though. A year later a different kind of storm came, and this one almost did us in. We had stood in faith for so long and had been patient. The pressure was immense, and we almost lost our desires and dreams for several months. However, through prayer, we held on and stood stronger than ever before. Now we have much of that series of dreams fulfilled. We look back and thank God every day that we did not give up. I urge you not to look at something else or give up once God gives you a desire and dream. It's worth standing and waiting for.

MAKE THE CHOICE TO WIN

I have poured my heart out to you in the pages of this book. I have shared some very personal experiences that my wife and I have had. You have seen how we were able to overcome difficulty because of the power of God within us. We let that power rise up in us and bring us through some very trying times in our lives. I believe that our personal experiences will somehow minister to you and allow you to see what course of action we chose when times were not so pleasant. I shared them to let you know that we won, because we desired to win. And through these personal experiences that we have had, you can see that when you have the decision to make, you won't need to find excuses to give up, but you can make the choice to win.

Living in the New Dimension is more than just a catchy little charismatic phrase. Life as God lives it is a realistic and attainable goal that is not for everyone but you. God's best can truly manifest itself in **your** life. You can tap into this power source wherever you are and achieve as much as you can believe God for. Make the decision to take the Word of God, allow it to come alive within, and become the Unlimited You.

Books By Don Clowers

The Power of God's Character

A look at the relationship between the fruit of the Spirit, the nine spiritual gifts, and the five ministry gifts.

$5.25 Each

Spiritual Growth

A guide to help you reach beyond your present stage of maturity and continue to grow spiritually each day.

$3.95 Each

BOOK AND TAPE LIST BY DON CLOWERS

SINGLES: $4.00

21017A . . . . . Stand Up And Live
31002A . . . . . Wait, Renew, Mount-Up, Walk, Run
31211A . . . . . If It's Going To Be It's Up To Me
40226A . . . . . Overcoming Failure
40325A . . . . . The Importance of Regular Fellowship
40408A . . . . . Push Forward, Break Out, Go Over

TWO TAPE ALBUMS: $8.00

30724A . . . . . Position, Power, Purpose
31106A . . . . . I Want My House Back
10308A . . . . . How to End Your Money Problems
11213S . . . . . The Anointing
20512A . . . . . Weeds or Flowers

THREE TAPE ALBUMS: $12.00

10222A . . . . . Limited or Unlimited
31130P . . . . . Intercessory Prayer
30602P . . . . . The Diligent Shall Rule

FIVE TAPE ALBUM: $20.00

11011A . . . . . God is No Child Abuser

SIX TAPE ALBUM: $24.00

30105P . . . . . The Christian Family

Item	Price	Quantity	Total
		Total	

Terms: Check or Money Order only. Do not send cash. Full payment must accompany all orders.

Don Clowers Ministries, Inc.
P.O. Box 21389
Chattanooga, Tennessee 37421